K–6

Accidental Techie
to the Rescue!

Simple Tech Solutions for Your
Biggest Classroom Challenges

Lori Elliott, EdD
"The Accidental Techie"

Crystal Springs
SDE BOOKS

A division of Staff Development for Educators
Peterborough, New Hampshire

Published by Crystal Springs Books
A division of Staff Development for Educators (SDE)
10 Sharon Road, PO Box 500
Peterborough, NH 03458
1-800-321-0401
www.SDE.com/crystalsprings

© 2012 Crystal Springs Books
Robot illustrations © 2012 Crystal Springs Books

Published 2012
Printed in the United States of America
16 15 14 13 12   1 2 3 4 5

ISBN: 978-1-935502-27-2

e-book ISBN: 978-1-935502-29-6

Library of Congress Cataloging-in-Publication Data
Elliott, Lori, 1968-
    Accidental techie to the rescue! : simple tech solutions for your biggest classroom challenges / Lori Elliott, EdD.
        pages   cm
    Includes bibliographical references and index.
    ISBN 978-1-935502-27-2
    1. Educational technology. 2. Internet in education. I. Title.
    LB1028.3.E435 2012
    371.33—dc23
                                                                2012001990

This book is dedicated to all of the incredible teacher friends I've made throughout the years. Thank you for inspiring, challenging, and encouraging me.

Contents

Acknowledgments

A very enthusiastic thank you goes out to my incredible editors, Sharon Smith and Diane Lyons. It was an absolute pleasure to work with the two of you again. I really appreciate all the encouragement and wisdom you both provide. I'd also like to extend my appreciation to Jill Shaffer Hammond for the wonderful design work. I love it. I'm so grateful to Staff Development for Educators, especially Terra Tarango and Lisa Bingen for the opportunity to share my ideas in another book.

To my precious family, Tim, Austin, and Ashlyn: thank you for your love, encouragement, and humor. I'm so blessed to be surrounded by such a caring and supportive family. Thanks for always urging me to try new things and to share what I've learned. Your jokes and positive attitudes get me through every situation.

I'd like to express my gratitude to the teachers who have shaped my understanding and practice. To Dr. Beth Hurst, thank you for giving me the opportunity to work with your students so many years ago. Who could have known that it would be the beginning of a whole new world for me? You are such an inspiration to me! I also want to thank Julie Phelps and Ruth Henslee, my eMINTS trainers. The two of you helped me to understand and fall in love with technology.

I'd also like to thank Paula Armknecht and Jen Mueller for graciously allowing me to share their WebQuests with you here in this book. There was space to run only one of them, but these wonderful ladies are my friends and colleagues at the Nixa Public Schools, and they both deserve a special mention for all their incredible work with WebQuests.

Introduction

Years ago my principal presented me with an opportunity to receive extensive technology training and equipment for my classroom. As ironic as it sounds now, I actually turned it down. I told my principal no. I really thought my students would be better off creating things from scratch and conducting research using the hundreds of books I'd accumulated over the years. Boy, have I kicked myself a zillion times over the years for that poor decision.

But life sure does unfold in funny ways. Perhaps it was precisely because of the hasty manner in which I turned down that opportunity that just a few months later I found myself wondering: could technology improve my teaching and engage my students in learning? In a style that's very characteristic of me, I decided to jump, head first, into exploring that question.

First off, I noticed that students needed more options for learning and creating. More and more of the conversations among them seemed to be technology-driven. They compared notes about their video game scores, cell phones, and what they were reading online. Markers, poster board, and Play-Doh weren't cutting it anymore. As I searched for answers I took a realistic look at my classroom setup. My classroom only had one computer, so I brought in my own laptop and borrowed old machines from relatives. I literally started playing with this idea of technology integration.

It wasn't easy. I didn't know how to make a PowerPoint presentation, and I'd never heard of a WebQuest. But I knew the students would help me along the way, and they did. We learned together. I figured out how to structure our day so that everyone could take turns and rotate through the computers. I could have Internet access on only one computer, so we had to juggle things. Honestly, it wasn't long before I was hooked and realized I wanted more for my students.

I also took a hard look at myself and how I was using my time. I often felt overwhelmed with all the tasks in front of me. I started to wonder if I could use technology to simplify my day-to-day teacher duties. Could technology help me to communicate more effectively with parents, organize my materials, grow professionally, and build an even stronger classroom community?

Trying to find the answers to those questions led me to new discoveries. By accident I'd end up finding resources and web tools while looking for other things. When I was assigned the task of creating the end-of-the-year fourth grade slideshow, I went online and learned how to edit videos. It seemed that one accidental discovery would lead me to another, and I got hooked. Luckily for me, about a year after I started trying to figure out this whole technology thing, another opportunity to attend training to learn how to create a technology-infused classroom with lots of solid instruction and equipment opened again. This time I fought for the chance.

It's Worth the Investment

Over the years, I've found there really is a difference when I use digital tools in the classroom. Not only have I observed a higher level of engagement among my students, but I've seen the quality of their thinking increase. It's true that integrating technology in the classroom does take an investment of time at the start, but as your knowledge base grows, so does student engagement. In fact, your students will likely be the ones best equipped to help you on your journey, so let them. I have no problem asking my students for help and ideas. Teachers learning from students may not be the traditional approach, but it provides students ownership of their learning, and it builds a community of respect and trust.

Accidental Techie to the Rescue!

Identifies

Provides
Tech Solutions Aligned with NETS-S

Real Life
• Problems
• Challenges
• Needs

Practical, Step-by-Step Guide to Tech Tools, Strategies & Practices

Immediate Improvements for both
Teachers Students

I'm excited for you to begin your journey. If you're a little over-whelmed about the whole process, I understand. But I promise this will be painless. Please let me, the Accidental Techie, come to your rescue. The tools I've chosen to include in this book are some of my very favorite resources. They'll help you enhance your learning environment and reenergize your instruction.

How to Use This Book

This book is organized into two sections. The first section shows you how to use technology to enhance your learning environment; the second section offers ways to use technology to reenergize your instruction.

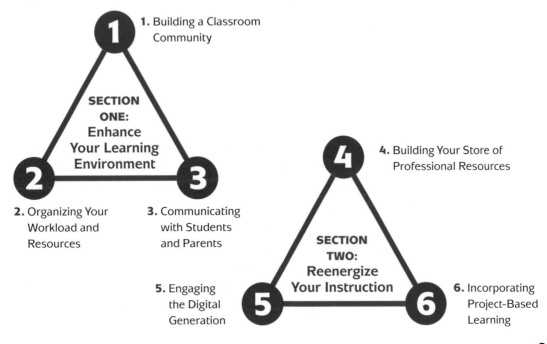

1. Building a Classroom Community

SECTION ONE:
Enhance Your Learning Environment

2. Organizing Your Workload and Resources

3. Communicating with Students and Parents

4. Building Your Store of Professional Resources

SECTION TWO:
Reenergize Your Instruction

5. Engaging the Digital Generation

6. Incorporating Project-Based Learning

Each chapter focuses on a common classroom challenge. I've provided three or four different solutions to help you meet each challenge. Each solution is a tech tool that's free and easy to use. In order to make learning the technology as simple as possible, I've structured each chapter in the following way:

Let's Get Started: Here's where I walk you through how to use each tool step-by-step. I've included lots of pictures so you can see exactly what I'm talking about. My goal is to get you comfortable and confident enough to use the tool in your classroom right away.

Look What You Can Do: Here's where I'll kick your skill level up a notch. Once you have a basic understanding of how to use a particular tool, you'll learn how to use it in your classroom, using some of its more advanced features.

Get Real: Are you the kind of person who just needs to get near a computer and stuff seems to go on the blink? Relax. In this section I've tried to troubleshoot all of the problems you may encounter using this technology.

A Quick Tip: Here's a bonus for you after you've read the rest of the section. This is one really neat takeaway that you can grab in an instant.

Dip Right In

I understand how busy you are. This book has been designed so that you can learn about each tool independently of the others. If you're facing a particular challenge right now, then flip right over to that section of the book and let me help you. If you like to read things from start to finish, I hope you'll enjoy the journey. Please don't feel like you need to use every tool offered. I don't want you to feel overwhelmed. Instead, take a look at your options and choose the ones that best meet your interests and needs.

Track Your Own Progress

We all use rubrics and other assessments to track our students' growth. Why not track your own progress? I've also provided you with a Technology Continuum. Whether you're still getting covered in Vis-à-Vis pen color each day while you roll out the overhead projector or you're looking like a pro while your students create amazing things online, everyone has room to grow, including me! You can use it to assess where you are right now with technology and the challenges you face. Later, come back and see where you are on the continuum after you have tried a few things.

Technology Continuum

Read through the statements below. Make the selection in each row that best describes you at this time. Keep track of your points to determine your current techie level.

1 POINT	2 POINTS	3 POINTS
I'm scared of technology. I'm afraid I'll break something.	I like technology, but I don't feel very confident.	I love technology and love to try out new things.
My idea of integrating technology is to show a video.	My idea of integrating technology is using digital media and websites to catch my students' interest.	My idea of integrating technology is to seamlessly use technology tools throughout my instruction and have students use technology tools to show their understanding.
I'm not sure we need to use so much technology in our classrooms. Kids just want to be entertained.	I know I need to use more technology to engage my students, but I'm not sure how to do that. What do I do if it doesn't work?	I realize our students are digital natives, and they want to be engaged with learning in a real way. Technology doesn't amaze them; they just expect it.
I've never used a web tool. What is that anyway?	I've tried a few fun web tools, but I'm not sure how that translates into the classroom.	I use web tools daily for instruction and as a way for students to create.
I feel overwhelmed with all of this new stuff, and the training at school was nonexistent or limited.	I'm uneasy because I haven't had time to play with the tools I have, and the training I received was limited.	I spend lots of time playing with new tools and have found they get easier to use the more I use the technology.

What's Your Techie Level?

If your total is 5–7, you're a Newbie Techie. You see technology and teaching as two separate worlds. This book can help you understand why technology can be a valuable teaching tool.

If your total is 8–11, you're a Techie on the Move. You believe that technology and teaching should go together, but you might not feel confident in your ability to implement new technology in your classroom. This book can help you enhance your skills and confidence.

If your total is 12–15, you're a Techie Teacher. You believe that it's all about the teaching, not the tools. That said, you strongly believe that technology tools enhance instruction and learning. This book should offer you new ways to expand on how you bring technology into the classroom.

Enhance Your Learning Environment

Building a Classroom Community

Do me a favor. Take a few moments to think about your favorite teacher. Why is this person so memorable? Why do you remember some teachers and classes with fondness while others make you cringe? I really believe it usually stems from the type of classroom community present in those learning environments. My middle school social studies teacher was tough, but she treated each of us with respect. She listened to what we had to say. Her smile was magical. She would listen, grin, and then tell us how smart we were. My second grade teacher understood that a class that sings and plays together stays together. She shaped my philosophy of teaching, and I can't imagine a day in my own classroom without a fun song and a good book.

Taking the time to create a safe, positive, and, yes I will say it, *fun* classroom community is important. Here's what I've found from my own classroom. When I make it a priority to help my group of students bond as a team or as a family, I notice that academic achievement increases as well. I've also found that classroom behavior is more appropriate; students have better attitudes about learning; and they even treat one another better. Why is that?

Create a Positive Classroom Community

When you boil it all down, learning comes back to relationships. When Marc Prensky interviewed thousands of students for his book, *Teaching Digital Natives: Partnering for Real Learning*, he asked them, "What do you want from school?" One of the consistent answers was that students want to be respected, trusted, and have their opinions valued and count for something. I see the need for positive and cooperative classroom communities throughout that statement.

I bet our favorite teachers all understood that building a classroom community is an ongoing process. It takes a daily commitment to create an environment where students value themselves and others, where they feel emotionally safe enough to take academic risks, and where they view school as a great place to be.

Use Technology in a Meaningful Way

This chapter is all about providing you with technology resources to assist you in building your classroom community. I'll discuss using Survey Monkey to gather information about your students, Smilebox to create class slideshows, and Voki to help even the shyest child share. Our favorite teachers didn't have access to all of the cool technology that we do today, but if they had, I'm sure they would've agreed with what I always stress about technology: you can have all of the latest and greatest tech tools in your classroom, but if you don't use them to connect with students in a meaningful way, then the technology is worthless. The one thing students still desire and need is a positive relationship with their teacher and their peers. In the following pages, I'll be showing you ways to incorporate these tools into your classroom to enhance your teaching and student learning.

SOLUTION 1

Gather Data with Survey Monkey

Isn't the beginning of school the most exciting time of the year? There's just something about purchasing bright and shiny school supplies and getting your hands on your new class list. The urge to decorate bulletin boards takes over. Seeing those curious and eager faces walk in the door the first day is priceless. Reality soon sets in when we recognize that each of these cherubs has his own set of hobbies, interests, likes/dislikes, learning styles, and backgrounds.

As good teachers, we know that if we can figure out what makes our students tick, we can use that in our instruction to make learning relevant. This generation of students is most comfortable with technology, so how about having them take an online interest inventory to gain insight into each of their personalities? Survey Monkey will help you create great-looking surveys in no time, and if you choose 10 or fewer questions for your survey, you won't have to pay a dime for the service.

As the year progresses, use Survey Monkey to create pre- and post-assessments. You can view the responses of an individual student or the general responses of the whole class. Then use the data you collect to select books, create lessons, and provide anchor activities that directly address your students' knowledge levels, interests, and learning styles. Talk about differentiated instruction!

Let's Get Started

In order for students to actually take the survey you create using Survey Monkey, it's helpful to have access to a district-provided webpage, a classroom website (see pages 69–79 for setting one up), or a blog. If you don't have these tools, see the Get Real section of this chapter for an alternate method.

GET AN ACCOUNT

1. The first step is to go to http://www.survey monkey.com/ to set up your free account. Look toward the bottom right of the home page and click on the *Sign Up FREE* button.

2. Choose a username, password, and enter your e-mail address.

3. If you'd like to receive e-mail information from Survey Monkey, leave the box checked beside the phrase *I'd like to receive communications . . .*

4. If you'd rather not receive these updates, uncheck this box. When you're finished, click on the yellow *Sign Up* button.

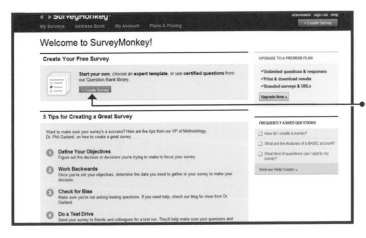

CREATE YOUR SURVEY

1. Once you've created your account, you'll see the welcome screen. Click on the *Create Survey* button.

2. You're going to create a new survey, which is the preselected choice.

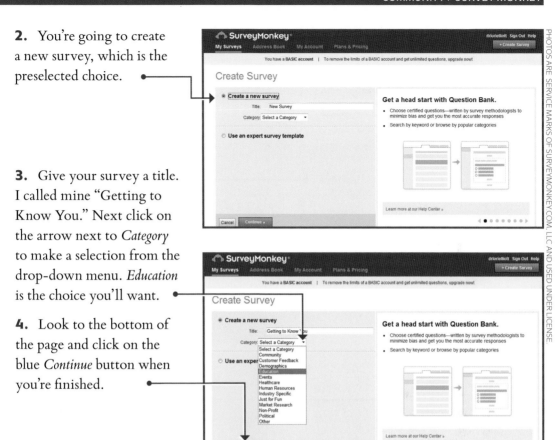

3. Give your survey a title. I called mine "Getting to Know You." Next click on the arrow next to *Category* to make a selection from the drop-down menu. *Education* is the choice you'll want.

4. Look to the bottom of the page and click on the blue *Continue* button when you're finished.

CREATE YOUR SURVEY TEMPLATE

1. Now, you'll actually construct the survey. Notice you're on the *Edit Survey* page. Your first choice is to change the look of your survey by selecting a color theme.

2. Click on the drop-down arrow next to the word *Aqua* to choose a color. The color you select here will appear across the top of the screen in your finished survey.

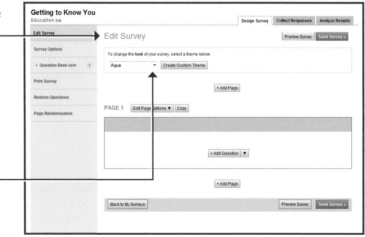

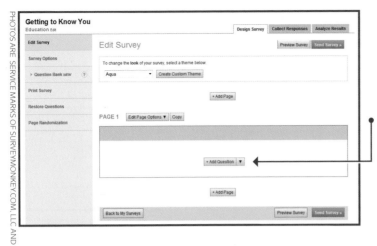

3. Once you've selected your color, you're ready to start typing in the questions for your survey. Look at the middle of the page and click on *Add Question*.

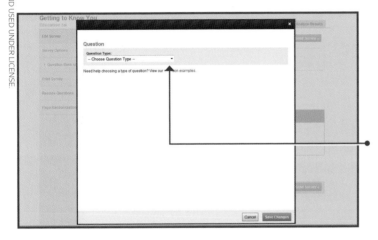

CHOOSE YOUR TYPE OF QUESTION

1. The new window that opens will prompt you to select your type of question. Click on the dropdown arrow next to *Choose Question Type* to view your options.

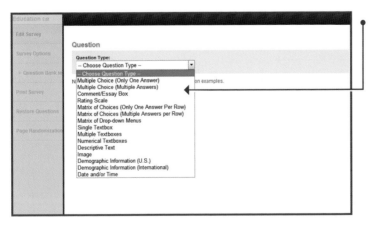

2. Most often I choose the *Multiple Choice (Multiple Answers)* option. I try to include only a few *Comment/Essay Box* questions. Students would rather click from a list than write out a long answer, especially at the beginning of school.

3. If you select a multiple choice option, you can have the answers display in one column or in more than one column. Click on the drop-down arrow next to *Display Choices As . . .* to make your selection.

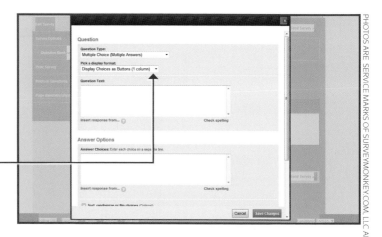

WRITE YOUR QUESTIONS

1. Now it's time to write your first question. Click on the box labeled *Question Text* and type in your question.

2. When you're done typing, you may want to click on the *Check Spelling* feature under the text box. Handy!

3. Next, you'll enter each answer option on a separate line in the *Answer Choices* box.

4. Scroll down and look under the *Answer Options* box. You'll see some optional features. To allow students to be able to fill in their own answers if none of the choices you provide works for them, then click on the box that says *Add "Other" or a comment field*.

PHOTOS ARE SERVICE MARKS OF SURVEYMONKEY.COM, LLC AND USED UNDER LICENSE

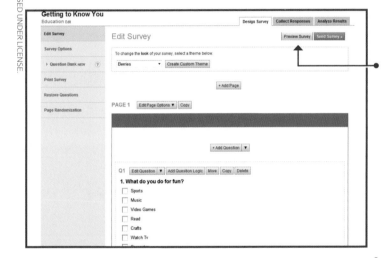

5. When you're done, go to the bottom right-hand corner of the screen and click on *Save Changes*.

PREVIEW YOUR WORK & ADD MORE QUESTIONS

1. You'll be taken back to the *Edit Survey* page. Want a sneak peek at what you've done so far? Look at the top right-hand side of the screen and click on the gray *Preview Survey* button.

2. A new window will pop up showing you how the survey will look when your students see it. To close out of the preview, go to the top right-hand side of the screen and click on the gray *Exit This Survey* button.

3. You'll be brought back to the Edit Survey page. Continue to build your survey by clicking on the *Add Question* button. Remember, you can write up to 10 questions for free. Each time you enter a question and a set of answers, click on *Save Changes*.

MAKE YOUR SURVEY AVAILABLE

1. Once you've entered your final question and clicked on *Save Changes*, you'll be back on the Edit Survey page.

2. Take a look at the top right-hand side of the screen. You'll see three tabs: *Design Survey, Collect Responses*, and *Analyze Results*. Click on the *Collect Responses* tab to choose how you'd like to make your survey available to students.

3. On the *Collect Responses* page, you'll see four choices. You can create a *Web Link, Email* the survey, embed the survey to a *Website*, or *Share on Facebook*.

4. Since most students don't have their own e-mail addresses, and they shouldn't have Facebook accounts, those two options are out. The remaining options are to link or to embed the survey to a website.

5. What's the difference? A link would make a "click here to take the survey" type of message appear on your site, and the embed option would place the survey directly on the site.

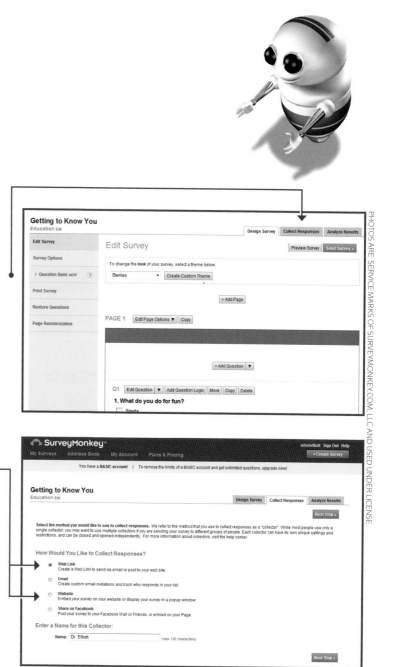

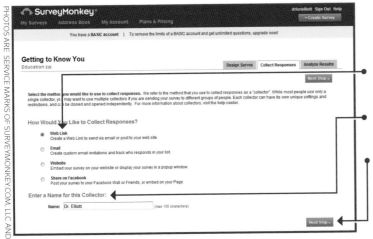

CREATE A WEB LINK

1. To create a web link, click on the circle by *Web Link*. Then look down the page and find *Enter a Name for this Collector*. Type your name in the box, and then click on the blue *Next Step* button.

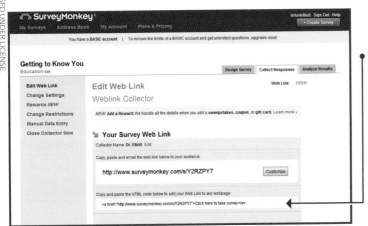

2. You want the html code provided at the very bottom of the screen. Copy and paste this code to your website. For instructions on how to link material to a website created on Weebly, see page 77.

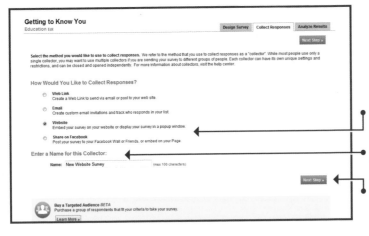

EMBED THE SURVEY

1. To embed the survey, click on the circle by *Website*. Then look down the page and find *Enter a Name for this Collector*. Type your name in the box, and then click on the blue *Next Step* button.

2. The next screen looks confusing. Just select *Embed* from the list of options and then click on *Save*.

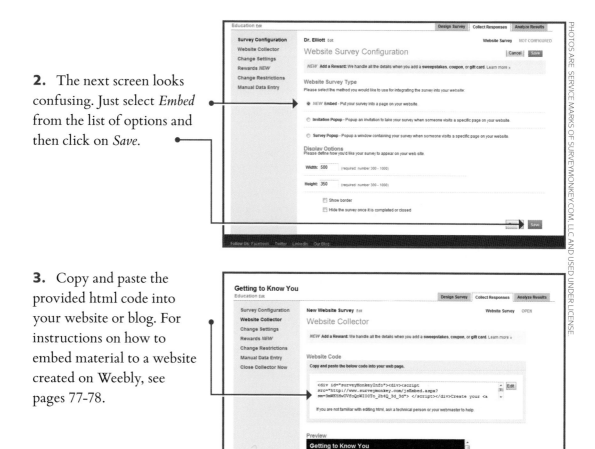

3. Copy and paste the provided html code into your website or blog. For instructions on how to embed material to a website created on Weebly, see pages 77-78.

VIEW THE RESPONSES

1. After your students take the survey, you'll want to view the results. Log onto your Survey Monkey account. At the top left, click on *My Surveys* and then click on the survey title you want to view.

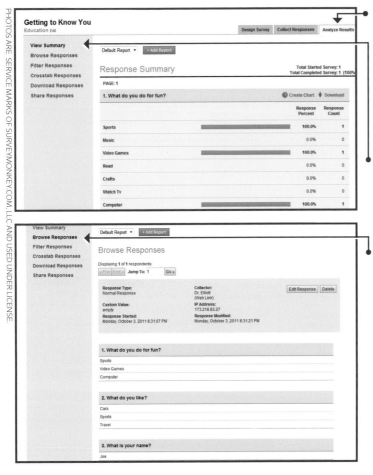

2. Once you've selected your survey, go to the top right of the page and click on the *Analyze Results* tab.

3. Look to the left-hand side of the screen. You'll see a menu of options. Click on *View Summary* to see the overall class results.

4. If you'd like to view individual responses click on *Browse Responses*. I always include the question, "What is your name?" on every survey so that I can identify each student's set of responses.

Look What You Can Do

You can use Survey Monkey to create surveys for parents, too. Ask parents to share information about their child's personality, likes/dislikes, family dynamics, goals they have for their student, etc. E-mail the survey to parents the first week of school or make it available on your website. Use the *Browse Responses* option to see the feedback from individual parents. Remember to ask for parent/guardian name and student name on the survey to help you identify each set of responses. This involves parents in the learning process, and it helps you to work as a team to best educate and support each student.

Get Real

In order for students to access the survey, you need to either link it to or embed it in your website or blog. But what if you don't have a website or blog? No problem. Instead, you can save the link as a *Favorite* on your computer, or as an icon on your desktop. To learn how to save the link as an icon on your desktop see page 43.

Survey Monkey is designed so that a survey may only be taken once on an individual computer. This can be a real problem if you're using the same computers for multiple students. There's a simple fix, however, you can make so this won't be an issue.

Log on to Survey Monkey and click on *My Surveys*. You'll see all of the surveys you've created in a list. Look across the page to the icon that looks like three people under the heading *Collect*. Click on this icon.

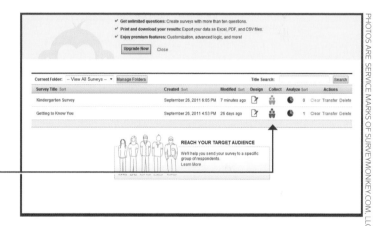

You'll now see a page that shows you the *Collector Name* or method you previously selected for how you wanted to share your survey. If you embedded the survey to your website, click on the blue text next to *Website Survey*. If you linked the survey, click on the blue text next to *Web Link*.

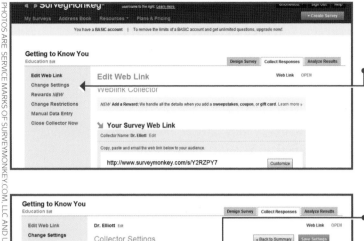

When the next screen pops up, look to the left-hand side of the page. Click on the *Change Settings* option.

Look under the first question, *Allow Multiple Responses?* and select the *Yes* option. Click on the blue *Save Settings* button, and you're good to go. Everyone can take the survey without any hassles.

A QUICK TIP

Survey Monkey's professional templates can save you time. Click on *Create Survey* to start a new survey, and then click on the *Use an expert survey template* option. You can choose from a list of categories, including education. These templates have statements and questions already prepared; just customize them to meet your needs.

SOLUTION **2**

Create Slideshows on Smilebox

Years ago families and friends gathered together to watch slideshows of vacations or old photos. Remember slide projectors? They had those round carousel trays filled with individual slides. When you hit the button on the machine, the wheel of pictures would move one step forward dropping a slide into the projector. It was a noisy and cumbersome process, but it was the only way we had for everyone to see the same picture together on a big screen.

Thankfully, watching slideshows today is not only easier, it's also more entertaining. We can add music and interesting transitions to our pictures. But why would we watch slideshows in the classroom? We watch for the same reasons that you and your family or friends sat around your living room watching, talking, and laughing about your memories. When we share pictures of things we've experienced as a collective group, we build a stronger sense of community. The experience brings us closer together because we remember the fun we've had together or the things we've done as a group. Using slideshows really does send the message, "We're all in this together," and all of our students want to feel that they're part of a group that cares about them.

Smilebox is an online tool that allows you to create slideshows. You can share the slideshows in class and post them online for parents to see. The process of making a Smilebox creation is a piece of cake. I find it actually relaxes me. I just know you're gonna love all of the great options they have for backgrounds and music. So, gather everyone together and grab some popcorn. It's show time!

Let's Get Started

You'll need to sign up online for Smilebox and then download the Smilebox software to your computer. The process is free and easy, but if you're downloading to your computer at school, you may need a technician to help you with this because it's unlikely you have permission to download a program onto your computer.

Once you have Smilebox downloaded to your computer, you'll be able to access your work by clicking on the Smilebox icon saved to your desktop. Smilebox saves your work to your computer, which means you can work on and view your slideshows without Internet access if you've saved your work. Of course you won't be able to use newly added Smilebox features or send slideshows through e-mail until you are connected to the Internet again. I know you're really curious now, so let's get going.

DOWNLOAD SMILEBOX

1. Zip over to http://www.smilebox.com/. When you arrive at the home page, click on the *Get Started* button.

2. If you're using Windows 7, you'll have a bar at the bottom of the page that asks if you want to *Run* or *Save* the Smilebox setup. Choose *Run*.

3. If you are using an older version of Windows or a Mac, you may see a box that appears on the screen asking if you want to allow Smilebox to make changes to your computer. Click on *Allow.*

4. The next window that appears is the *License Agreement*. Read through the terms of the service.

5. You'll probably want to uncheck the choices under the terms that make Smilebox your home page and default search engine and add Smilebox tools to your toolbar. When you're ready, click on the *I Agree* button.

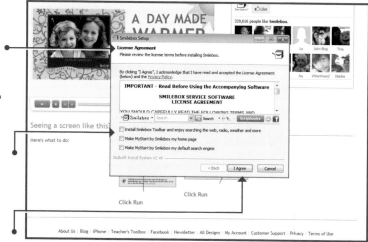

SET UP AN ACCOUNT

1. Now that you've agreed to let Smilebox load their software to your computer you'll need to create an account.

2. To create your Smilebox account you'll need to type in your name, e-mail address, and a password. Click on the *Create Account* button when you're finished.

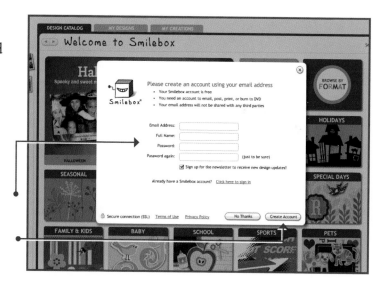

CREATE YOUR WORKSPACE

1. Once your account is created, you'll be taken to the *Design Catalog* tab. Notice your name will be in the top right hand corner of the screen.

2. On the lower left-hand side of the screen you'll see buttons labeled *Get Photos* and *Get Video Clips*.

3. In the middle of the screen you'll see all the different theme categories for slideshows and other templates.

UPLOAD PHOTOS

1. Let's upload some photos. Perhaps you'll choose pictures from the first day of school or ones that highlight the cool science experiment you did yesterday. Whatever pictures you want to use will have to be ones you've saved on your computer.

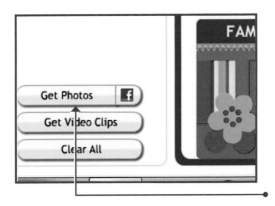

2. Look to the lower left-hand side of the screen and click on the *Get Photos* button.

3. The next screen that appears will display your *My Pictures* folder on your computer. If the images you want to use have already been saved there, the next step will be a snap.

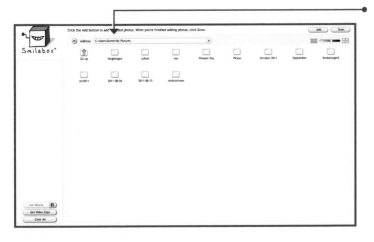

4. If you haven't saved your photos to your *My Pictures* folder, then you'll need to find where you've saved them.

5. To do this, click on the down arrow to the right of where it now says *Users> Owner> My Pictures* to open a drop-down menu. Find the location on your computer where you saved the pictures. Double click on the folder containing your pictures.

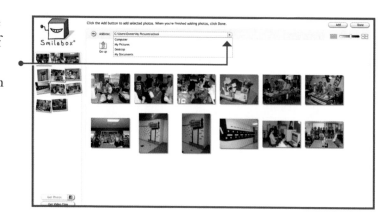

6. To select a photo, click on it. A pop-up menu will appear. Click on *Add*.

7. The picture you selected instantly appears in your workspace on the left-hand side of the screen. Continue, in this manner, selecting all of the photos you want to use in your slideshow.

8. Once you've selected all of your pictures, click on the *Done* button in the upper right-hand corner.

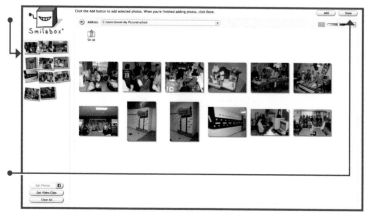

CHOOSE A FORMAT & THEME

1. It's time to choose your format and theme. This is the fun part, but there are so many options.

2. Click on the big *Browse by Format* button on the right-hand side of the screen.

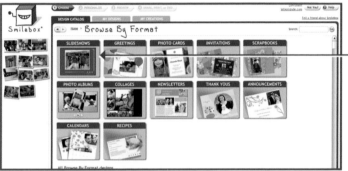

3. You'll see many format options to choose from, such as *Collages*, *Slideshows*, and *Photo Albums* just to name a few. Click on the format you like best. I chose *Slideshows* for this example.

4. A new screen will open to show you your theme options. You'll notice themes such as *School*, *Seasonal*, and *Holidays*. Click on the theme you like best. I chose *School* for the example.

5. The next window will show you all of the template options for that theme. To see a quick preview of any template, click on it. When you've found a template you like, go to the bottom of the preview window and click on the *Personalize* button.

6. This will download the template to your account so you can personalize it.

PERSONALIZE YOUR SMILEBOX

1. You're now on the *Personalize* tab. This is where you'll add text, edit your photos, and add music to your Smilebox.

2. Depending on the template and format that you've chosen, your next set of options will vary. I'll go over the basic editing options used in a *Slideshows* template.

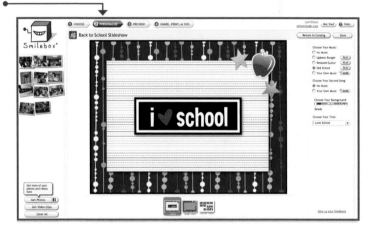

3. No matter which format you choose, I'm confident that you'll find Smilebox is very easy to use.

PERSONALIZE A SLIDESHOW TEMPLATE

1. The first slide you'll probably see under the *Personalize* tab is your Intro Slide. Look under the large photo box. Click on the *Slide View* button. You'll see your first slide appear in the photo box.

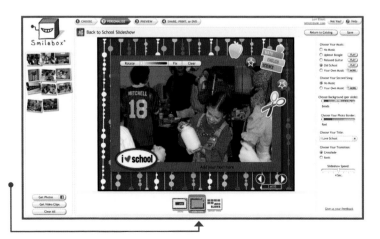

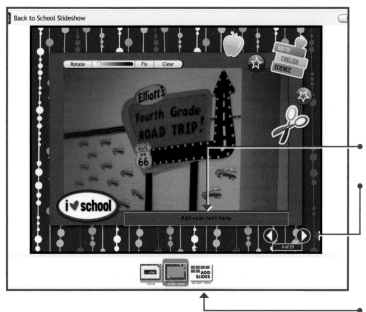

2. To add a caption to any picture, click on the *Add your text here* box and type. To proceed to the next slide, click on the right facing arrow. It's typically located toward the bottom of the photo box.

3. If you'd like to add more slides, click on the *Add Slides* button found under the photo box.

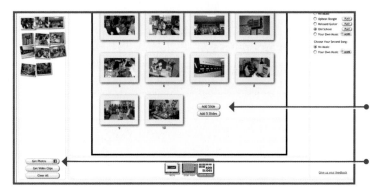

4. Two options will appear on your screen. Click on either *Add Slide* or *Add 5 Slides* and then click on the *Get Photos* button located on the bottom left-hand side of the screen.

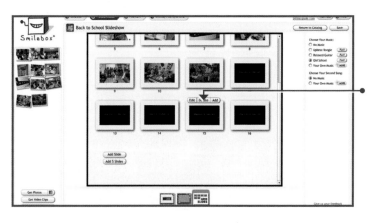

5. If you don't want to use all the slides provided, just click on an empty slide and select *Delete* from the pop-up menu.

6. To change the order of your pictures, just click and drag the individual photos around to place them in the order you want.

7. Look to the right-hand side of the page. Smilebox provides several free music choices. To preview a choice, click on a *Play* button.

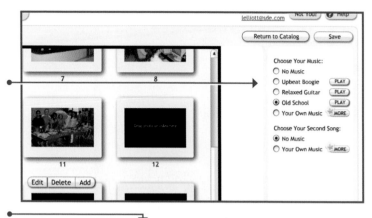

PREVIEW THE SHOW

1. Ready for a sneak peek? Look at the tabs on the top of the screen. Click the *Preview* tab. Once you're finished previewing, click the *Esc* key on your keyboard to get back to your project.

2. If you like your show, then look to the top right-hand side of the screen and click on the *Save* button.

3. A pop-up window will appear asking you to name your creation. Type in the name and then click *Save*.

4. If you want to make more changes you can stay on the *Personalize* tab and continue to work. When you're done, click on *Save*.

SHARE YOUR SMILEBOX CREATION

1. How do you want to share this creation with others? If you're just showing

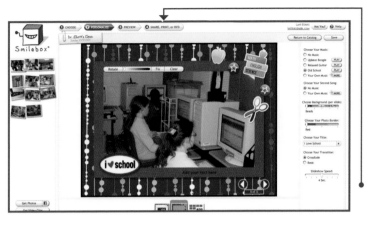

it to your class, then you can play the saved Smilebox creation straight from your computer.

2. If you want to share your Smilebox creation online, click on the tab at the top of the screen that says *Share, Print,* or *DVD*.

3. When you click on this tab, a new window will pop up with more choices. To e-mail the show to parents, look under the *Email Your Creation* option and click on *Send*. A window will open for you to type in the e-mail addresses.

4. To post the show to your website, blog, or Facebook class page, click on *Post*.

5. Give your creation a name, and then click on *Continue*.

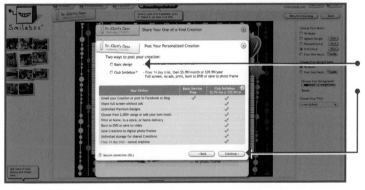

6. Since you're using the free version of the site, click on the circle next to *Basic Design* and then click on *Continue*.

7. Look at the tabs on the top left-hand side of the screen. To post your creation to Facebook, click on the Facebook icon. To post to your website or blog, click on the last tab that says *More*. The html codes needed to embed or link your show will appear on the right side of the screen.

8. What's the difference between linking and embedding? A link would make a "click here to view the Smilebox" type of message appear on your site, and the embed option would place the Smilebox slideshow directly on the site.

9. To embed it, copy and paste the html code to your site. To link it, copy and paste the URL provided to your site. For instructions on how to link and embed material to a website created on Weebly, see pages 77–78.

REVIEW YOUR OPTIONS

1. After sharing your show, you may want to preview it again or edit the presentation. To get back to your main account, look at the top right-hand side of your screen and click on *Return to Catalog.*

2. To see any templates you've personalized or downloaded, click on the *My Designs* tab. To see the projects you've completed or are still working with, click on the *My Creations* tab to the right.

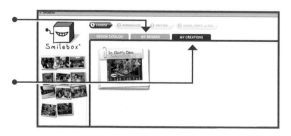

Look What You Can Do

Consider showing an end-of-the-week slideshow each Friday to remind students not only of the fun they've shared but the learning that has been accomplished. After viewing the entire slideshow, watch it again and stop at various times to have students discuss the key concepts they learned while those photos were taken. This can be a much more entertaining way to review. The brain stores information based on pictures so using slideshows provides students with hooks for their own learning and remembering.

A QUICK TIP

Smilebox offers full-time teachers the opportunity to receive a free one-year subscription, which allows you to take advantage of all the Smilebox features. Click on the Smilebox Teacher's Toolbox at the bottom of their home page and register for your free account.

Get Real

Make sure you're clear about your school's policy regarding posting student pictures to the Internet. Give parents the chance to opt out of having their students' pictures posted.

If your district doesn't allow you to post student pictures, you can still make and share Smilebox creations with your class because the photos aren't online. They will have been created and saved only to your computer.

SOLUTION 3

Communicate Using Voki

If you could be any cartoon character who would you most like to be? I'd choose Wilma Flintstone. She wears a really cute dress and cleans her house while wearing pearls. That's my kind of gal. Cartoon characters have always captured our attention. These days we can create cartoon-like characters online that are meant to represent ourselves. These characters are called avatars. People can talk, share ideas, and compete using avatars. Maybe you have a Wii gaming system. If so, you've probably created an avatar to represent yourself while you play the games.

Voki is an online site that allows you to create a talking avatar for free. With Voki, you can create your own character, tell it what to say, and publish the character giving your message. Voki is a wonderful tool for both teachers and students.

You and your students will have such a fantastic time creating and using these avatars, which offer students a way to communicate with others without the fear of public speaking. Provide Voki as an option for students to use when they share research findings, give book reports, or describe how to solve a math problem. Helping our students to gain confidence and feel like an important part of the group is what we're striving for in building our classroom communities. When students take ownership of their learning, attitudes and motivation improve. Cartoons aren't just for Saturday mornings anymore.

Let's Get Started

To understand the process of creating an avatar using Voki, I'm going to lead you through creating a character of your own. Then you'll be able to show your students how to create their own Voki avatars.

SIGN UP FOR AN ACCOUNT

1. Zip over to http://www. voki.com/ to get started. To set up your free account click on the orange button that says *Get Voki*.

2. Type in your name, e-mail address, password, and birthday. Read the *Terms of Use* by clicking on those highlighted words. If you agree, check the box and click on the *Sign Up* button when you're finished.

3. A pop-up window will appear telling you to check your e-mail for a confirmation message. Go ahead and do that.

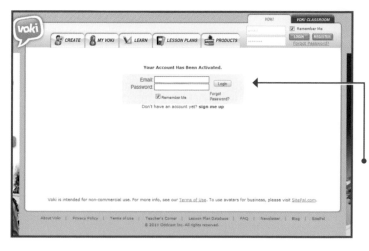
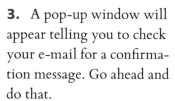

4. When you click on the activation link in your e-mail, you'll be brought right back to Voki. Log in to get started.

CREATE A CHARACTER

1. You'll be taken to your Voki account page. To make your own avatar, find the blue tab titled *Voki For My Site* and click on the gray *Create a New Voki* button.

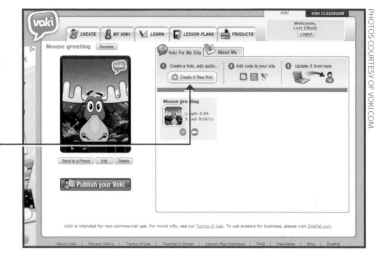

2. You'll see a default Voki character presented in a box on the left-hand side of the page. You'll be able to change almost everything about this character.

3. Notice to the right of the Voki character the choices available to you to customize your character. You should see *Customize Your Character*, *Give It a Voice*, *Backgrounds*, and *Players*.

4. Under the character, you should see a box with color options allowing you to change the color of its mouth, eyes, skin, and hair.

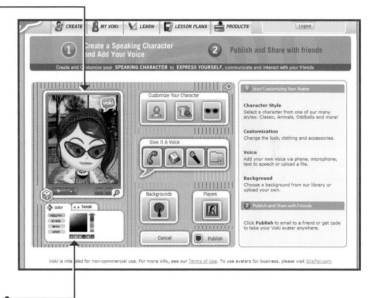

CUSTOMIZE YOUR CHARACTER

1. Let's start with the *Customize Your Character box*. Click on the small icon of the person in that box and a new window will open.

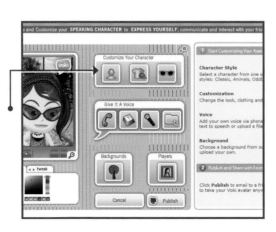

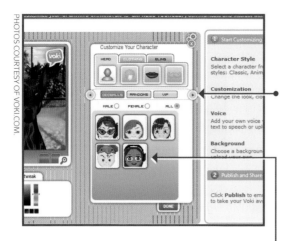

2. Now, carefully look right below the icon that you just clicked on. You'll see a menu of character types. Use the left and right arrows on either side of the menu to scroll through the list of types.

3. When you click on a category, a display of character options opens in the box below the menu. When you find the character you want to use, click on it.

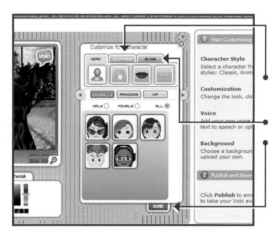

4. If you want to dress your avatar, click on the *Clothing* tab. To add accessories like jewelry, click on the *Bling* button. Click on *Done* when you're finished adding features.

GIVE YOUR CHARACTER A VOICE

1. Let's make this avatar talk! Look in the middle of the screen and find the *Give It A Voice* box. You have four choices.

2. My favorite is the *Text-to-Speech (TTS)* feature. There's just something really cool about hearing the words I've typed spoken in another voice. Students find this more fun, too.

3. To type your message, click on the icon of the keyboard key with the letter *T*. When you're done typing, look under the text box to see options for choosing the language and voice you want your avatar to speak.

4. To preview your work, click on the *Play* button after you've typed your words. The play button looks like the sideways arrow under the text box. Click on the green *Done* button when you've finished typing.

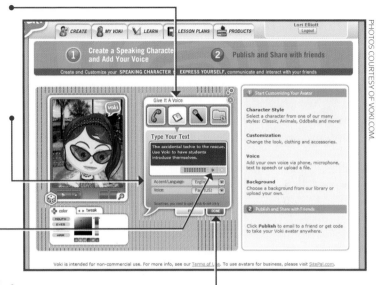

ADD FINISHING TOUCHES

1. Your avatar is looking good and sounding smart. If you'd like to change the background for your avatar, click on the *Backgrounds* box. It's the one with the *Tree* icon on it.

2. See that frame around your character? It's called a player. If you want to change the color of your player, then click on the *Players* box and make your selection.

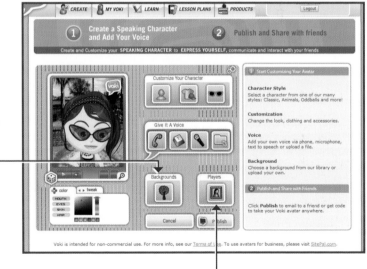

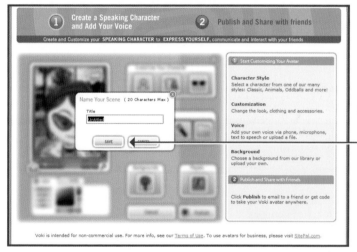

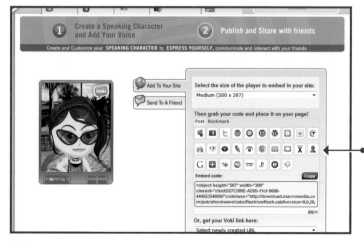

PREVIEW & PUBLISH

1. Make sure to preview your avatar and its voice by clicking on the button with the sideways arrow all the way to the left of the Voki player, near the die.

2. When you're pleased with all your changes it's time to publish. Look to the bottom right of the page and click on the gray *Publish* button.

3. A new window will appear, and you'll be prompted to *Name Your Scene*. Give your Voki a title, and then click on the *Save* button.

SHARE YOUR CHARACTER

1. Goodness, you have so many choices for how to publish this adorable character. Each of the icons you see represents a different place that you can share your Voki avatar.

2. But I want you to look below those options. To embed your Voki character to your website, copy that long html *Embed Code* by clicking on the blue *Copy* button. Next, you'll need to paste this code to your website.

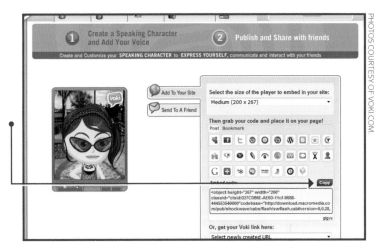

3. For instructions on how to embed material to a website created on Weebly, see pages 77–78.

4. If you'd rather link your website to your Voki (which means you'll have a "click here to see my Voki" type of message instead of the actual Voki), then click on the down arrow next to *Select Newly Created URL*.

5. A pop-up window will open. Click on the *Standard Voki Link* option.

6. Voki will provide you with a web link. Copy and paste the link to your website. For instructions on how to link material to a website created on Weebly, see page 77.

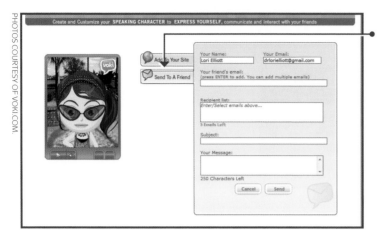

7. You can also e-mail your Voki. To do this, click on the *Send To A Friend* tab and enter in each recipient's e-mail. You can e-mail your Voki to up to five people at a time.

8. Does this beat being Wilma Flintstone? You know how much fun you had creating your avatar. Think about the fun your students will have when they create their own characters.

Look What You Can Do

Use your Voki avatars to introduce lessons, give announcements, provide directions, and share messages during your class meetings. You can also use Voki to announce the Student of the Week or provide compliments to the class or to specific students. The novelty of using the avatars immediately pulls students in to listen, especially if you use one of the unique accents provided. The Australian one cracks me up, mate.

More importantly, think of all the ways you can have students use Voki. At the start of the school year, ask student to introduce themselves using Voki avatars. Voki is a valuable tool for our shyest students because it helps them share successfully. Consider having a different student each week make a Voki to summarize the week's activities. You can also place the Voki on your website for parents to enjoy. For more ideas on how to

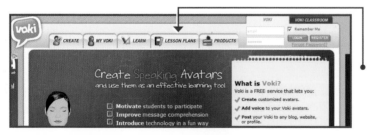

use Voki in actual lessons, check out Voki's free lesson plan database. On the Voki site, click *Lesson Plans* at the top of the page.

Students can view the Voki in class several different ways. You can project it onto an interactive whiteboard or screen using an LCD projector and the computer. Students can also view the

Voki on an individual computer by clicking on the link you've added to your classroom website or blog. Don't have a website or blog? Then you can bookmark the Voki link to your computer or save it to your desktop as an icon.

Creating an icon is super easy. Go to your computer desktop. Right click anywhere on the desktop. (If you have a one-button mouse, hold down the control key and click.) A pop-up menu will open. Roll your mouse over the choice *New*. When the next menu opens, click on *Shortcut*.

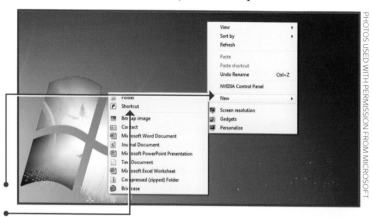

A pop-up window will open. Type or paste in the link and choose *Next*.

In the next window that appears, type in the name of the icon, such as Voki. Click on *Finish*.

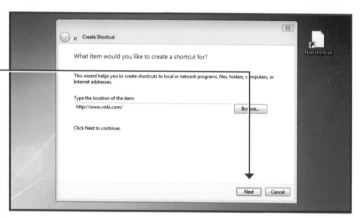

Now you have an icon on the desktop for students to use. Isn't that awesome!

Students can create their own Voki by using the free account you've created. Have everyone in your class use the same account so you can see what each student is doing. This will also prevent students from needing to have their own e-mail addresses to register. If you want all of your students to

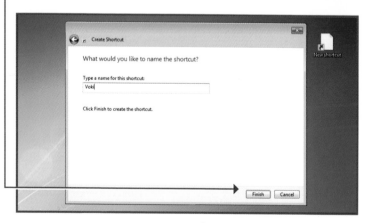

work on Vokis at the same time, you may want to create more than one account for them to use to prevent delays. Usually one account for every

PHOTOS USED WITH PERMISSION FROM MICROSOFT

five students is sufficient. If you need to, you can create multiple e-mail accounts in Google Mail or Yahoo mail.

Get Real

Can't you just see students getting off-task with this one? Creating an avatar is so much fun that it's natural for students to want to play around. To get the best results and save valuable time, make sure students write out a script for their character before going to the computer to create the avatar. This will make the process go more smoothly and help keep students on task.

Many districts have strict Internet policies because online safety for students is a big concern. A plus to using Voki is that no student images are used. And, if you use the text-to-speech feature, then student voices aren't being shared either. This may be a relief to some parents who are a bit nervous about having their student's work online. The Voki avatars are pretty much anonymous, so there's much less worry about online safety.

How will students ever learn public speaking skills? Voki is a neat tool, but it will never replace face-to-face communication. It can be used to bring novelty and fun to assignments and activities, but, of course, you'll want to continue to assign oral presentations, lead discussions, and spend valuable time together as a class.

A QUICK TIP

English language learners can use Voki avatars to practice and listen to their speech. They may use the computerized voice first and then record their own voices when they feel more comfortable. It's a great way to practice writing, reading, and pronunciation.

Organizing Your Workload and Resources

When I first started teaching 20 years ago, I was known for a lot of things: running an active classroom, teaching interesting thematic units, and using real books instead of basal readers. The other thing I had a real reputation for was being disorganized. My classroom always looked like it had just been hit by a strong wind. The maintenance folks hated my room, and I'm pretty sure I wasn't at the top of the secretaries' favorites list either. I never could put my finger on the things I needed, and I was always behind in getting paperwork turned in. I'm certain the office manager let out an audible sigh each time she searched through the stack of important documents, and, once again, mine was nowhere to be found. Where in the world was that stinkin' piece of paper? Maybe it was underneath the folders, or the books, or the papier mâché, or the dioramas. Who knew?

Well, I knew I had to change my ways. I mean how many times did I have to purchase the same bulletin board set at the local teacher store just because I couldn't find the one I bought three months ago? Once I finally got serious about organization, it saved me a lot of time, money, and stress. I'm a reformed disaster area. What made the difference? Honestly, it was technology that started making my life easier, my use of time more efficient, and my paperwork more streamlined.

Make a Clean Sweep

Before putting digital tools to work, my first step toward rehabilitation of disorganization was to take a good look around my classroom and honestly assess how often I used the things sitting on the shelves or the furniture cluttering my space. Then I did the most painful thing for a teacher, I purged. The funny thing about teachers purging their classrooms is that after we put our throwaways in the hallway, somebody else takes the stuff to her room. I guess one teacher's trash is another's treasure. By the time I was finished, I had eliminated worn-out books, old resources, and lots of bulletin board borders. I felt so relieved, and things really looked spiffy in my classroom.

Create a Virtual File Cabinet

But chaos was still lurking in that old metal monster called my file cabinet. Paperwork is a nightmare for most of us. We have documentation for everything: plans, worksheets, tests, parent newsletters; the list goes on and on. The good news? This is where technology can really help shake things up. You can go digital. One day it hit me like a ton of bricks. Why in the world was I keeping all of that paper in a file cabinet I rarely used. It was a classic case of out of sight, out of mind. I discovered online web tools that could streamline my to-do list, strengthen my collaboration with colleagues, and categorize all my school pictures. I had no need for that file cabinet, so out it went.

Technology is meant to make our lives easier. There are a lot of great resources to help you reduce clutter and get focused. In this chapter I'll share two of my favorites to help you clean house. Dropbox and Shutterfly can help you to store and share your most precious resources online. Sound like a plan? Now, if I could just get those closets at home cleaned out. Is there an App for that?

SOLUTION **1**

Access & Share Files with Dropbox

Once upon a time there was a teacher who spent hours putting together some fabulous presentations to share with her colleagues in another state. She was balancing school, family, and the upcoming trip so she took a short cut and only saved those gems to her flash drive. I know you can see the writing on the wall, but hang in there. She rushed to the airport after school, caught a late plane, and finally plopped herself in the hotel room at close to 11:00 p.m. Feeling so confident, in fact pretty cocky about the great work she had done, she decided to double check those presentations just one more time so she would look like a pro the next day. To her surprise and horror those presentations were nowhere to be found. The flash drive device had somehow erased everything, and she was left with nothing ready for the conference except a cute outfit and fresh pedicure.

So what did this dear friend of mine do? She stayed up into the wee hours recreating those entertaining PowerPoint presentations. So, boys and girls what can we learn from this sad tale? We need to back up our documents. Relying on one or two storage places can be risky, as our beloved heroine discovered. She knew better, but everyone makes mistakes.

With the development of "cloud computing," the term for saving things online by using various web tools, you no longer have to rely solely on your computer, a flash drive, or an external hard drive. As long as you have Internet access, you can access any of your documents, pictures, etc. no matter where in the world you are! Cloud computing can save you from sleepless nights and wasted time. One of the most popular sites in the cloud is Dropbox. Let me show you how its magical powers can help you get organized.

Let's Get Started

You'll need to sign up online for Dropbox and then download the Dropbox software to your computer. The process is free and easy, but if you're downloading to your computer at school, you may need a technician to help you with this because it's unlikely you have permission to download a program onto your computer.

DOWNLOAD DROPBOX

1. Dropbox is a free tool that provides you with up to 2 GB of storage space, which really is a very decent amount of space. If you find later that you need more space, there's a nominal fee.

2. To get started go to http://www.dropbox.com/ and click on the blue *Download Dropbox* button.

3. A pop-up window will open asking if you want to *Run* or *Save* the file. Click on *Run*.

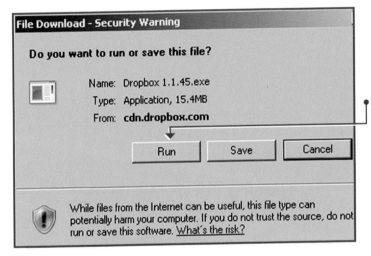

4. After Dropbox begins to run and set up the program, it will ask you if you want to allow Dropbox to make changes to your computer. Click on *Yes*.

5. The next step is to actually install the program. When you see the *Welcome to Dropbox Setup* window, click on the *Install* button.

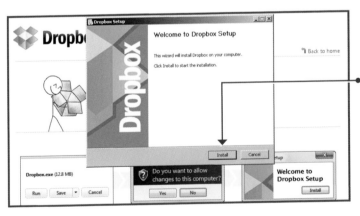

SET UP YOUR ACCOUNT

1. Now that you've installed Dropbox, you need to set up your account so you can access it online, as well as on your computer. Select the first choice that says *I don't have a Drop-box account* and then click on *Next*.

2. To set up your account you'll need to enter your name, e-mail address, a password, and your computer name, just to identify the computer that you're on. Name it something simple like, "Lori's Computer."

3. Read the *Terms of Service* by clicking on those highlighted words. If you agree, check the box and click on *Next* to continue.

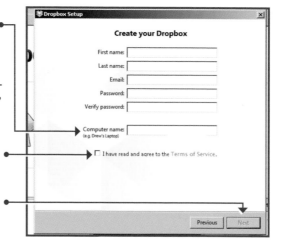

4. You'll be asked to select the Dropbox size you're planning to use. Most of us will be happy to use the 2 GB for free. If you ever find yourself needing more space, you can always add it later. Click on *Next*.

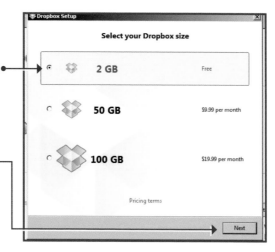

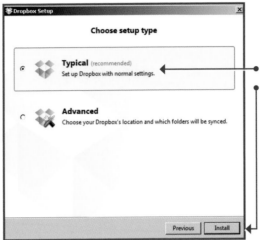

5. The next step is to tell Dropbox what type of settings you want. Click on *Typical* and then click on *Install* at the bottom corner of the screen. This is finalizing the set-up process.

6. A pop-up window will open offering you a *Tour*. If you'd like to take the tour, click on the big blue arrow. Otherwise, click on *Next*.

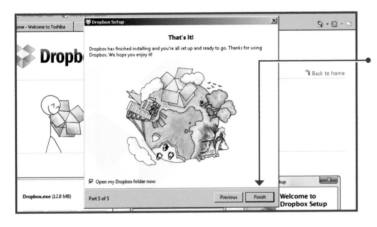

7. A final pop-up window will appear telling you that you're good to go. Click on *Finish*.

SET UP AND SAVE TO YOUR FOLDERS

1. Your Dropbox account is now created, and you'll see it in front of you. Notice you have a *Photos* folder and a *Public* folder. You can add more folders by clicking at the top of the screen where it says *New Folder.*

2. Once you've added a new folder you'll want to give it a name. To do this, click on the words *New Folder* and type in the name you want.

3. You can now place copies of documents or files into their appropriate folders in your Dropbox account. I'll show you two different ways to do this.

METHOD #1: USE YOUR MOUSE

1. Let's say that you have a photo from your Fourth Grade Pioneer Day saved to your computer that you want to place in Dropbox.

2. Right click your mouse on the Pioneer Day picture on your computer and select *Copy* from the pop-up menu. If you have a one-button mouse, hold down the *Control* key and then click.

3. Now place your cursor on the icon of the folder in Dropbox where you want to save the picture. Right click your mouse again, and choose *Paste* from the pop-up menu.

METHOD #2: GO TO FILE> SAVE AS

1. Now let's try another approach. This time I'll show you how to save a PowerPoint presentation (PPT) that's on your computer to Dropbox for backup. First, double click on the PPT to open it.

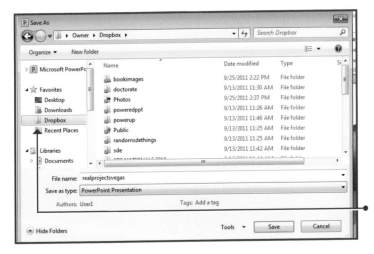

2. Next click on *File* and then click on *Save As*.

3. Look on the left-hand side of the pop-up screen to see your options for where you can save your PPT. Double click on *Dropbox*.

4. Now you must locate the folder in Dropbox where you want to save your PPT. If you don't have a folder already created, click on *New Folder* and create one.

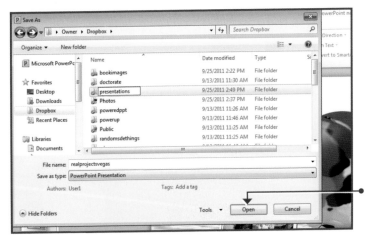

5. If you had previously created an appropriate folder, choose that folder by clicking on it, and then click on *Open* at the bottom of the screen.

6. Look at the top of the window. It should now read *Owner> Dropbox> Presentations*. Since you want to save your PPT in the *Presentations* folder of Dropbox, click *Save*.

7. Now you can access your PPT from Dropbox from any computer, anywhere in the world.

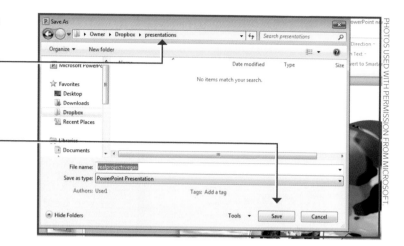

HOW TO ACCESS YOUR DROPBOX FILES

1. If you're on your computer you can view all of the folders in your Dropbox files by double clicking on the *Dropbox* icon on your desktop.

2. To access those same files when you're on another computer, go to http://www.dropbox.com/. At the very top right-hand side of the screen in small letters is a *Log in* button; click on it.

3. Fill in your e-mail address and password, and then click on the blue *Log in* button. Ta-da! You now have access to all of your files saved in Dropbox. No more recreating a lost document in the wee hours of the morning.

Look What You Can Do

You can use Dropbox to share files with colleagues. Teachers often work together in grade-level teams within a school or in district-wide teams to create curriculum materials, PowerPoint presentations, parent information packets, etc. Imagine how helpful it would be to have these kinds of files easily accessible to all of the members in your team.

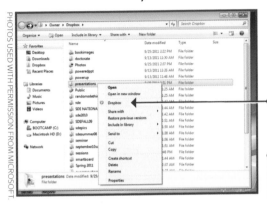

Sharing files using Dropbox is simple. When you right click your mouse on a folder in your Dropbox account, a menu will open. (If you have a one button mouse, hold down the *Control* key and then click.) Find and click on the word *Dropbox*.

You'll see two options: *Browse on Dropbox Website* or *Share this folder*. Click on *Share this folder*.

The next screen gives you the opportunity to type in the e-mail addresses of those with whom you want to share this folder. You can even write a message describing the folder or whatever you want to share.

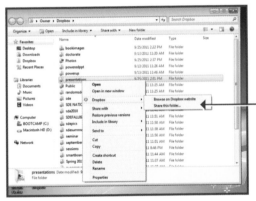

The people you invite to share your folder will receive a message by e-mail. They can accept the invitation to share.

If they accept your invitation and also join Dropbox, you'll get more storage space on your account. This is a nice perk to sharing folders. Now you and your colleagues have access to the same folder. You can all add or delete things. Make sure you share only with those whom you can trust. This is much easier than playing e-mail tag. Anytime anyone makes changes to the folder, all who are sharing will have instant access to the updated files.

Get Real

The only bump in the road I have encountered with using Dropbox is the potential to use up all my free storage space. Then I either have to delete items or pay for more space. Picture, video, and music files are large, so I use my Dropbox mostly for Word documents, pdf files, and PowerPoint presentations to help with the space issue.

The other possible problem with sharing folders is that others may add too many items to your folder or delete items that you wanted to keep. Be choosey in selecting which folders you share and with whom. In your message of invitation, make clear your expectations for how you'd like the folders managed. I recently opened one of my shared folders and found some video clips I'd never seen before. It took a little investigating to track down which colleague had accidentally added those videos to our professional file. It wasn't a big deal, but it reminded me how easy it is to lose control of my folders if I don't carefully choose the other users who are sharing access to the account.

A QUICK TIP

Dropbox also has a music player. Did you know that? You can save your favorite classroom music files and then play them using the DropTunes site. How awesome would it be to have your playlist for writing time and brain breaks right at your fingertips? Log in at https://droptun.es/login with your Dropbox username and password and listen to your own music playlist saved in your Dropbox account.

Share Pictures on Shutterfly

Not so very long ago when I'd want to share photos of a recent field trip or science fair with students' families, I'd have to tape the pictures to my newsletter and then run off copies. The black and white results weren't too spiffy. And I remember the effort I'd put into creating those end-of-the year memory books for each student. I'd spend gobs of money to make extra copies of pictures and then spend days cutting and gluing to complete each student's book. It was a real labor of love!

Thank goodness for digital cameras. Taking and sharing photos is easier than ever. But now that you can take so many pictures, what do you do with them? How do you organize your pictures so you can find the ones you want to use? How do you share them with students and parents so they can have copies of their own?

One of my favorite photo sites is Shutterfly. It offers teachers the opportunity to set up a Classroom Share Site for free. It actually looks like your very own picture website. You can customize the look of your site and share it with parents. This is a great feature because it allows parents to view or download copies of the photos they want, saving you the expense of having the pictures printed. Digital still images and video also take up a lot of storage space on your computer, so it's nice to have a place online for you to store your school photos. I think you'll find that Shutterfly's Classroom Share Site is a perfect way to share your best classroom memories.

Let's Get Started

Right away, I want to assure you that the Share site you set up using Shutterfly will be a private site. The only people who can access the site must be invited personally by you. I really appreciate this type of security!

In order for parents to access your Classroom Share Site, you're going to need their e-mail addresses. A great time to request e-mail addresses is when you send out your back-to-school class information packet. Include a form in your packet that parents can fill out to provide you with their e-mail address. You'll also want to ask parents to give you permission to send them e-mails from Shutterfly. Be sure to let parents know that Shutterfly won't sell their e-mail address to another list or use it to send them spam. If people would prefer not to be included, of course don't input their e-mail addresses when you set up your class account.

Let parents know that by giving you their permission to send them e-mails from Shutterfly, they'll be able to add pictures and comments to your site as well as receive classroom event reminders. If you're not comfortable letting parents add pictures or comments to your site, then refer to the Get Real section of this chapter to learn how to control what your members are allowed to do.

GET AN ACCOUNT

1. First you'll need to go to http://www.shutterfly. com/ to register for a free account. Look at the very top of the page and click on *Sign up.*

2. Fill in your name, e-mail, and password. Read the *terms and conditions* by clicking on those high-lighted words. If you agree, check the box and click on the orange *Join now* button.

CREATE YOUR SITE

1. Next you'll see the welcome page. Scroll to the bottom of the page and click on *Create a site*.

2. When the new window opens, look for the box labeled *Classroom*. Click on the orange *Make a site* button in that box.

3. Now fill in the information about your page. Mark *Classroom* for the site category; select *Teacher* for your role; and enter your grade. When choosing a name for your site, try to name it something that'll be easy for parents to remember.

4. As you type in the name of your site, Shutterfly will instantaneously fill in the website URL to match. Jot down that web address. It's what you'll need to type in to access your site later.

5. The NCES ID is an optional feature to identify your school district. You can leave this blank if you'd like. When all of the information is filled in, click on the orange *Continue* button.

6. Next is the fun part. You get to choose the template for your finished class picture page. To see more options, click on the text choices written in blue above the templates.

7. Click on the template you like best, and then scroll to the bottom of the page and click on the orange *Create site* button.

SET UP YOUR CONTACTS & CALENDAR

1. You should now see a new page with your selected background. Here you have the option of letting Shutterfly guide you through the rest of the process. I suggest clicking on that orange *Yes, please guide me* button.

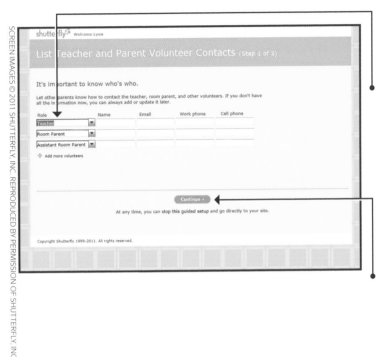

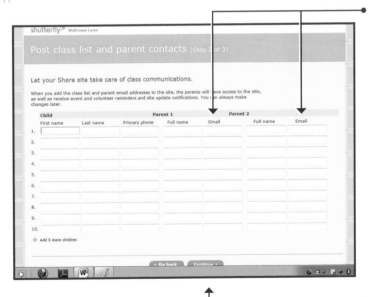

2. The window that opens allows you to fill in contact information about yourself, and, if you want, you can also share your room parent contact information.

3. The information you provide here will be made available to users of your site. It can be handy to provide this information, but how much and what you provide is completely up to you. Click the orange *Continue* button when you've filled in what works for you.

4. Your next option is to provide your class list and enter parent information. By entering parents' e-mail addresses you're granting them permission to view the site.

5. Entering the names of your students is entirely up to you. In most situations it's best not to identify students by name and certainly not by address or phone number. Fill in the appropriate information, and click on *Continue*.

6. If you'd like to use your new site to post calendar and upcoming event messages, then fill in this page. Of course, you can always come back and do this part later.

7. After completing the account set-up procedures, you'll see the *Congratulations!* page. At the bottom of this page, click on the orange *Take me to my site* button.

ADD PICTURES TO YOUR SITE

1. The next screen you'll see will display a pop-up window announcing that your site has been created. Click on the orange *Add pictures* button to begin uploading pictures to your Classroom Share Site.

2. Adding pictures is really easy. When the *Add pictures* window opens, notice at the top that you have the choice of adding pictures to a new album or an existing one.

3. Because you just got started, click on the circle next to *a new album*. Highlight the words "New Album" in the text box and type in what you'd like to call this album. Now look at the top of the window and notice the tabs. Click on the *Upload* tab.

4. Now it's time to locate and upload images saved on your computer to your new online album. Click on the gray *Choose files* button.

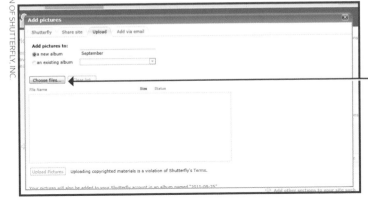

5. Your documents will appear in a pop-up window. Navigate to where you've saved your pictures. I save mine in a folder called *Pictures*. Within that folder I've organized my pictures into separate folders either by date or name.

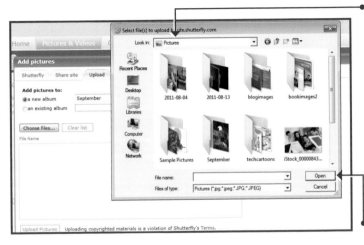

6. Double click on the folder containing your pictures, and then select the pictures you want to place on your site. Once you've selected the pictures, click on *Open*.

7. To select all of the pictures in a folder, click on the first image and then hold down the *Shift* key while you click on the last image.

8. To select just some of the images, click on one picture and then hold down the *Control* key while you click on each of the other pictures you want to use.

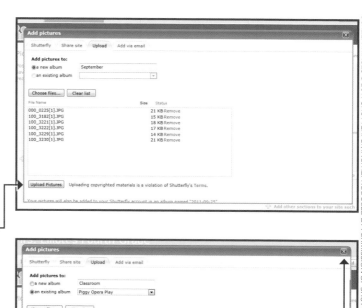

9. You'll see the list of pictures you've selected on the next screen. Click on the gray *Upload Pictures* button to complete the process.

10. It will probably take a few moments to upload your photos. Once the process is complete, all of your files will have a checkmark and the word "Complete" next to them. Click on the x at the top right-hand corner to close the window.

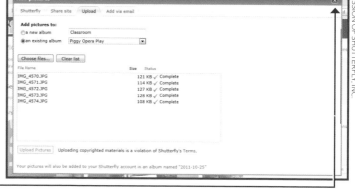

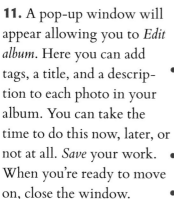

11. A pop-up window will appear allowing you to *Edit album*. Here you can add tags, a title, and a description to each photo in your album. You can take the time to do this now, later, or not at all. *Save* your work. When you're ready to move on, close the window.

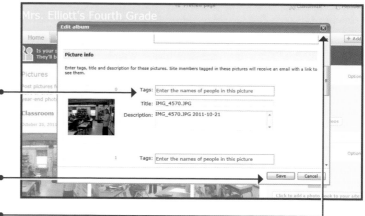

SCREEN IMAGES © 2011 SHUTTERFLY, INC. REPRODUCED BY PERMISSION OF SHUTTERFLY, INC.

12. Way to go! Take a few moments to admire your new photo album.

FINALIZE YOUR SITE

1. Let's check out your *Home* page. Look at the menu bar across the top of the page and click on the *Home* tab.

2. You can edit any section on your site by clicking on the word *Options*. A drop-down menu will open showing you all of the possible editing choices.

3. Take the time to visit each of the tabs listed across the top banner of your site: *Pictures & Videos, Calendar, Volunteer,* and *Class List & Contacts.* When you open a tab, you'll be able to click on the *Options* button to make changes.

INVITE MEMBERS

1. When you're pleased with your site, you'll want to send parents an invitation to view it. Look at the top of your *Home* page and notice the message written in blue across the page. Click on *Click here to send invitations.*

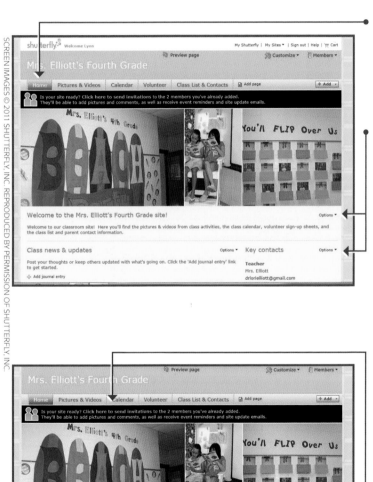

2. A pop-up window will lead you through the process of inviting members to visit the site. Click on *Send invitations* once you've previewed and edited your message. This will send the message to all the parents whose e-mail addresses you entered earlier.

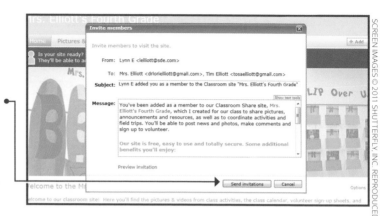

3. When parents click on the link provided in the e-mail Shutterfly sends, they'll be taken to your site. When they visit the *Pictures & Videos* tab, they'll be given the opportunity to copy, save, or order prints.

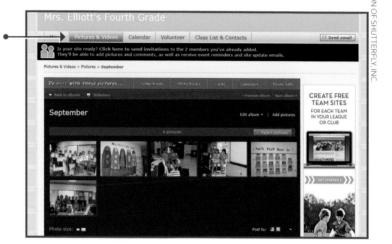

4. If people you haven't invited try to access the site, they'll receive a message that blocks them from viewing the page but encourages them to contact you if they'd like access.

5. Doesn't your site look amazing? Parents will really enjoy being able to see what's happening in your classroom on a regular basis.

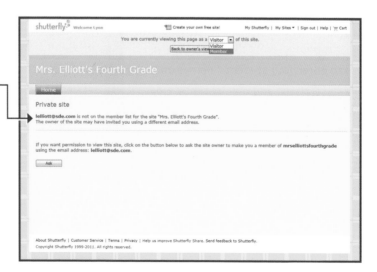

Look What You Can Do

Ask parent volunteers to create Photo Books using the pictures in your Shutterfly albums. When you upload photos to Shutterfly, you place the pictures in albums. You can then choose your favorite photos from each album and organize them into a kind of digital scrapbook, which includes text and collages that they call a Photo Book. These books are really wonderful. Photo Books can be posted on the site, and if others want to view or purchase the books, they have the opportunity to do so.

Make your load lighter by asking for a parent volunteer to help you maintain your Classroom Share Site. Many parents who work might be willing to take on this kind of project since they can do it from home and don't have to visit school to help.

Get Real

Before getting started, make sure you're clear about your school's policy regarding posting student pictures to the Internet. Be certain that you inform parents about your class site. Make them aware that only the families in the class will have access to the Classroom Share Site. Give parents the chance to opt out of having their students' pictures posted on this resource.

Not comfortable with letting parents comment on pictures, or add their own? Don't want members to be able to view each other's e-mails on the *Class Lists & Contacts* page? Then change the settings. You're in total control over what your members can view and access on your site. Shutterfly has preselected security settings that have worked really well for me over the years, but you may want to change them. Changing the settings is very simple. Just go to the page you'd like to edit and click on the *Options* tab. A drop-down menu will open. Select *Edit Section*. Click on the *Permissions* tab in the window that opens. Deselect the options you don't want parents to have access to and then click on *Save* when you're done.

A QUICK TIP

Help parents find their own students in images by tagging photos. On the *Pictures & Videos* tab, click on an album. Go to *Edit Album* and choose *Tag Pictures*. Here you can fill in the names of everyone in a picture. An e-mail will automatically be sent to the parents of the students tagged in the photos. Note that you will have to enter your students' names on the class list and their parents' email addresses.

Communicating with Students and Parents

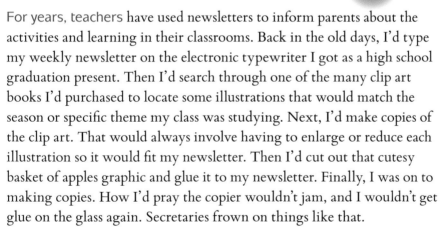

For years, teachers have used newsletters to inform parents about the activities and learning in their classrooms. Back in the old days, I'd type my weekly newsletter on the electronic typewriter I got as a high school graduation present. Then I'd search through one of the many clip art books I'd purchased to locate some illustrations that would match the season or specific theme my class was studying. Next, I'd make copies of the clip art. That would always involve having to enlarge or reduce each illustration so it would fit my newsletter. Then I'd cut out that cutesy basket of apples graphic and glue it to my newsletter. Finally, I was on to making copies. How I'd pray the copier wouldn't jam, and I wouldn't get glue on the glass again. Secretaries frown on things like that.

Of course that wasn't the last step in the process. Next I passed the newsletters out to students who had more important things on their minds, like recess. I'd watch like a hawk to make sure a pretty yellow paper went into each and every Michael Jordan or Little Mermaid backpack. I'd breathe a sigh of relief once that was accomplished—just to do it all over again the next week. The problem was, no matter how cute the snowman border on my newsletter was, there always seemed to be parents who had no clue what was going on in the classroom. They'd drop by to see me on Monday morning (of course!) when I was running around trying to get things ready for the week and question me about why I hadn't informed them of the field trip, Dr. Seuss Day, or whatever. I'd pull out my folder of newsletters and show them that all the latest and greatest news was covered in the most recent version of the *Elliott Times*. You know what came next. "My kid didn't get a newsletter." "I haven't seen one all year." Good grief. So much for parent communication.

Technology to the Rescue

Methods of communicating have changed radically. Many parents prefer receiving class updates through e-mail. Some would love to check up on today's classroom learning by checking their Facebook account. Still others like knowing there's a website to visit when they have a question. It's easy to understand why. We want to be connected to others all the time. We want whatever we need, whenever we need it, wherever we are. Facebook, Twitter, blogs, websites, and more make it easy to pass along important information, dates, and facts.

Realizing that the methods of communication have changed, we need to shift gears, too. If the newsletter isn't making its way home, it's time to try something else. You can still share the same information; you just have more options for *how* to share it. Now, when I have something exciting to let families know about, I put it on my blog or website. I then Tweet about it and post it on my Facebook class page. If I want to make sure someone in particular sees something, I e-mail it directly to that person.

You Can Do It!

In this chapter you'll learn how to step up your communication methods. Step-by-step, I'll walk you through how to create your very own classroom website using Weebly. I'll also show you how to go "paperless" with sign-up sheets using one of my favorite sites called SignUpGenius. You'll also learn how to set up a Facebook Organization page that parents can "Like." That way they can receive classroom messages from you 24/7. And it's time to put away your clip art books and glue. I'll show you how to create jazzy-looking newsletters on MailChimp that you e-mail to families so they're guaranteed to arrive. And did I mention that all of these online resources are free?

I promise this will be painless. Everyone will be so in the loop. There's only one problem. You might not have as many Monday morning guests, frantic e-mails, or phone calls. What *will* you do with all your spare time?

SOLUTION **1**

Create a Website with Weebly

More than ever, parents want to know exactly what's going on in the classroom. I've found that using only a monthly newsletter and a yearly parent-teacher conference just don't cut it anymore. Parents want access to information and updates at their fingertips. Providing a quality class website is a helpful tool in communicating with both parents and students. It allows you to post information that can be accessed 24 hours a day, 7 days a week. It can seriously lessen the clutter of paper and the number of frantic parent phone calls and notes.

A classroom website can be used to provide families with important information about your curriculum, upcoming events, assignments, and tests. It can be used to share enrichment or review resources such as websites and video tutorials to assist parents and students while they study at home. And if you keep your website current so it shows the learning taking place every week, it really helps build a strong sense of community.

Are you worried because you don't know the first thing about creating a website? Are you concerned about the cost and time? No need to fret. You can create a fabulous website using Weebly for free. Why Weebly? The designs look nice; the templates are incredibly easy to work with; and they don't place advertising on your site. Plus, they now have a special option for educators. Teachers can set up two free websites using Weebly.

Let's Get Started

The biggest question you have to answer before creating your website is, "Who's your audience?" Your answer should include parents and students. But it might also include other educators, administrators, and potential students. Your website will obviously serve as a way to communicate information to your audience. But it can also be a place where students go to access helpful links to educational websites and research materials.

Website Title: <u>Dr. Elliott's 4th Grade</u>

PAGE: MATH	PAGE: THE ELLIOTT TIMES	PAGE: OUR PHOTO GALLERY	PAGE: HELP-FUL MATH LINKES

Image/Information:
- Include welcoming comments and outline ways I hope families will use the site
- Include Class Picture

Take some time to map out your site. Having a plan in mind will make the creating part go much smoother. You'll certainly need to give your site a title, and you'll want to decide what and how many pages your site will feature. Add as many pages as you feel would be useful.

Think about the number of pages you'll need to link to your home page and what content you'd like to feature on each page. Perhaps you'll want a page for each of your subject areas, a page for newsletters, one for class photos, and one for helpful student links. Jot down the kinds of images and text you'd like to include on your home page. To help get you started, look at this sample template for a website's home page.

Page Title: _____

Elements I Want to Include on this page of the website:
- Include links to my favorite math sites including: Math Mayhem, Arcademic Skill Builders, National Library of Virtual Manipulatives

---

For each web page you want to build, create a template similar to the one shown here. Write down what you'd like to include on each page. Elements to consider include photos, text, documents, videos, and links to other websites. Now that you have a plan in mind, you're ready to get started!

CREATE AN ACCOUNT

1. The first step is to go to http://education.weebly.com/ and register for an account. You'll need to provide a username, password, and e-mail address. To read the *Terms of Services*, click on those underlined words. Then click on the orange *Sign Up* button.

2. Once you're logged in, you'll see your own page. You'll want to click on the *Add Site* button to create your website.

3. The next window that pops up will ask you to name your website and choose the type of site. Click on the arrow to open the drop-down menu. You'll want to select *Education*.

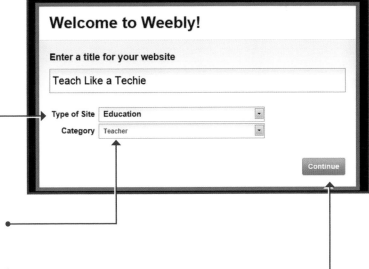

4. Another field will now open asking you to select a *Category*. Click on the arrow to open the drop-down menu again and choose *Teacher*. Then click on the orange *Continue* button.

CHOOSE A DOMAIN NAME

1. The next step is to give your website an address so students and parents will know where to find it. Try to use a name that'll be easy for everyone to remember.

2. The first option is to use an address with Weebly.com at the end. The second option is to customize your website, but that has a fee. So, let's stick to the freebie!

3. Type the name of your website into the box. Weebly will instantly let you know if the name you want to use is available. When you're done, click on the orange *Continue* button.

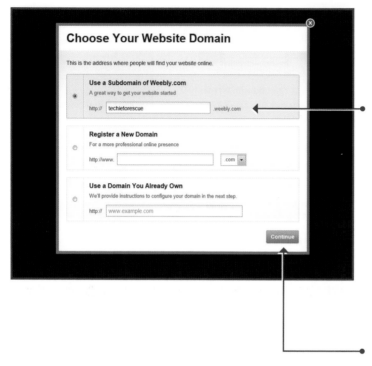

SELECT A DESIGN

1. Now it's time to get creative. Look at the blue bar across the top of the page. Click on the *Design* tab to see the different layout options for your home page.

2. If you want to see more choices, click on the white arrow with blue background found on the far right of the *Design* tab. Click on the layout that you like best to select it.

3. Scroll over the picture in the layout you just selected. An orange *Edit Image* button will appear. Click on this button if you want to replace this image with one of your own pictures.

INSERT YOUR OWN PHOTO

1. To insert your picture, click on the *Add Image* button. It's located on the upper left-hand side of the screen.

2. A pop-up window will open. Click on the green *Click to Upload a File from Your Computer* button.

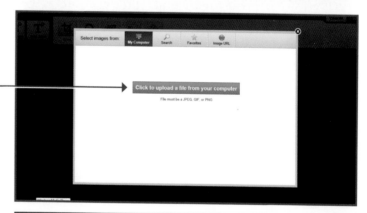

3. Find the folder where you save your images and double click on it. Click on the photo you'd like to select, and then click the *Open* button.

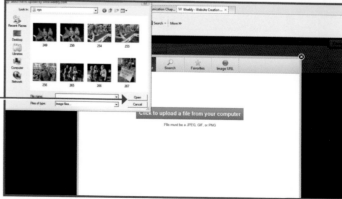

4. It'll take a minute to upload your picture, but once it's ready, you can click and drag anywhere on the picture to reposition it. You can also click on the *Crop* button to resize the photo.

5. When you're happy with how the photo looks, click the orange *OK* button. Now you can either upload more pictures or click on the orange *Save* button to continue.

CHOOSE YOUR ELEMENTS

1. Next you'll want to choose the elements you'd like to see on your home page. Think of the elements as the building blocks of your website.

2. Look at the blue bar across the top of the page. Click on the *Elements* tab and you'll see the different icon options. Click on the icon you want to use and drag it onto the page.

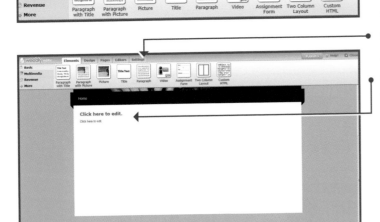

3. If, for example, you want a space to write a welcoming paragraph, click on and drag down the *Paragraph* icon. A *Click Here to Edit* message will appear. Click and start typing. So simple!

4. To see even more options, click on the *Multimedia* button located to the left of the *Elements* tab. Here you can easily add a *Photo Gallery*, *Slideshow*, *File*, and more to your page. Just click and drag the icon you want to use onto your page.

5. Let's say you'd like to display the latest class pictures. Click on the *Photo Gallery* icon and drag it to the page. A *Click Here* icon will appear; click on it.

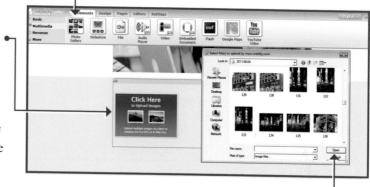

6. Find the folder where you save your images and double click on it. Select the pictures you want to include by clicking on each one. After selecting your photos, click on *Open*. This will place your pictures into the Photo Gallery.

7. To select all of the pictures in a folder, click on the first image and then hold down the *Shift* key while you click on the last image.

8. To select just some of the images, click on one picture and then hold down the *Control* key while you click on each of the other pictures you want to use.

ADD MORE PAGES

1. Just like one potato chip is never enough, neither is a one-page website. So, let's add more pages. How many? Refer back to the plan you made earlier. Don't worry if you don't know exactly how many pages you want. You can always add or delete pages later.

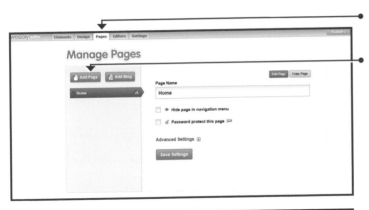

2. To add pages, click on the *Pages* tab and then click on the orange *Add Page* button.

3. Each time you click the *Add Page* button you'll create a new page. Give each new page a name. To do this, highlight and type over the words *New Page* in the text box.

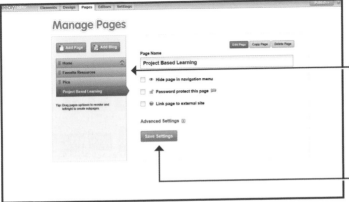

4. For example, I named my pages "Favorite Resources," "Pics," and "Project Based Learning."

5. After adding and naming your pages, go to the bottom of the screen and click on the orange *Save Settings* button.

6. Now you'll see your new pages added to the navigation bar on your website's home page.

7. To customize a new page, revisit the *Elements* tab and drag the components you want onto the page, just like you did with your first page.

HOW TO LINK MATERIAL TO YOUR SITE

1. When you link something, such as another website to your site, you're providing people a pathway to access the other site.

2. To add a link, click on the *Title* icon on the *Elements* tab and drag it to your page. A *Click Here to Edit* message will appear.

3. When you click on that message, a toolbar opens. Locate the icon that looks like links in a chain. That is the *Link* icon.

4. Type a message, such as, "Click here to play a great math game." Now highlight the text and click on the *Link* icon.

5. A pop-up window will open. Paste the URL, or website address that you want linked to your page into the *Website URL* option text box. Then click on the *Save* button.

HOW TO EMBED MATERIAL TO YOUR SITE

1. When you embed something to your website, you're placing that material directly on your site.

2. To embed something to your website, click on the *Custom HTML* icon and drag it to your page. A *Click to Set Custom HTML* message will appear.

3. Highlight the message and then paste in the long html code provided by the other site. Click on *Publish*. For examples of where to find html code on a website see pages 19, 33, or 41.

PUBLISH YOUR WEBSITE

1. After you customize each page, your last step is to publish your website. Look to the right-hand side of the screen and click on the orange *Publish* button.

2. A pop-up screen will appear asking you to select your website's domain. The choice ending in Weebly.com is the free one. Select it, then scroll down and click on *Continue*. Can you believe it? You're done!

3. Wow! That's amazing! You look like a rock star, and your readers are going to love visiting your incredible classroom website.

Look What You Can Do

Once you've established your website, you want students and parents to know where they need to go to get the latest and greatest news about your classroom. Make sure you refer to your website in all of your e-mails, newsletters, and parent nights. In a real sense, you have to train your readers to visit your site often, so plug it whenever and wherever you can.

When you're teaching a new unit, create a section on your website for students to use that's devoted to research links on that topic. Think of all the time you'll save in class. If the links are already prepared for students, then there's no need for typing in addresses, and students will stay focused on the learning instead of wandering to unrelated sites. Imagine how much more research, practice, or enrichment can be accomplished when everything is just a click away. Plus your students and their parents can access these same resources at home.

A QUICK TIP

The Weebly for Education site allows you to create accounts for up to 40 of your students to build their own websites free-of-charge. Instead of students doing reports or posters, they can use Weebly to create student web pages to show what they've learned. Click on the *My Students* tab to get started. You're in full control of your students' accounts and activity.

Get Real

Before creating a website, double check your district policy regarding what can and cannot be placed online. Even if you're not allowed to use photos of students, or their work, your website can still be chock-full of helpful information that will make it a valuable resource for students and parents.

If your district does allow you to use photos as long as the website is password-protected, then you might want to consider subscribing to the paid version of Weebly. When setting up your pages you'd want to select the *Password Protect* option before clicking the *Save Settings* button.

Involve Parents Using SignUpGenius

When I first began teaching, for whatever reason, I thought I had to do everything for my classroom by myself. I decorated the bulletin boards, made copies for upcoming assignments, bought supplies, and baked the cupcakes for the 100th Day of School. What was I thinking? Over the years, I found out that parents are often willing and able to help with many of the chores I was doing alone.

To keep great things happening in our classrooms, we need all the help we can get. When parents volunteer their time, supplies, or expertise, it's greatly appreciated. But the process of coordinating everyone's efforts can quickly turn into a not-so-fun game of telephone tag. Ditto that for parent-teacher conferences. The back and forth process of providing everyone with a timeslot that works with their schedule is enough to drive you crazy.

Why not put technology to work for us and cut down on the stress? SignUpGenius is just what it sounds like. It's a brilliant way to use the web to get people to sign up for just about anything. You create your sign-up form online and e-mail it to the parents. They simply click on a link in the e-mail to view your sign-up page. Then they make their choices by clicking on the options. You can immediately know who has signed up and for what. You can also have SignUpGenius send out reminders to help parents manage their time. Trust me. This will quickly become one of your favorite resources.

Let's Get Started

You'll need the e-mail addresses of the parents, and any other people, you want to send your sign-ups to. It's also a good idea to ask parents to give you their permission to send them e-mail messages using SignUpGenius.

I like to request this type of information in my back-to-school class information packet. If some people would rather not receive e-mails, of course, I don't include them in the list. Instead I provide them with a paper copy of the sign-up. Let parents know that SignUpGenius won't sell their e-mail address to another list or use it to send them spam.

SET UP AN ACCOUNT

1. The first thing you need to do is create a free account so you can manage your sign-ups. To get started go to http://www.signupgenius.com/. Look at the banner across the top of the screen. You'll see a row of green tabs. Click on the *Create a Sign Up* tab.

2. A new page will appear. Fill in your name, e-mail address, and password to set up your account. After filling in the information, click the orange *Submit* button.

3. Awesome! Now you're ready to get things going. The next screen you'll see is the *Create a Signup* page. This is where you'll create the document that will be sent out in an e-mail to parents.

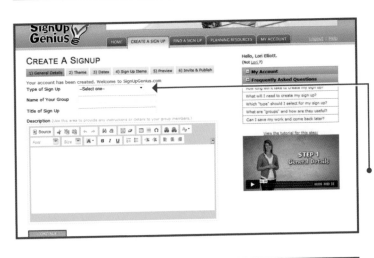

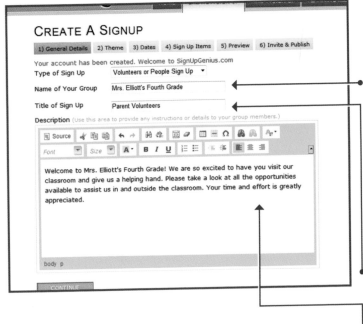

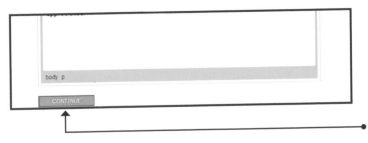

CREATE A SIGN-UP

1. Your first choice is to select the *Type of Sign Up*. Are you looking to create a sign-up for volunteers or do you want people to bring in food? Click on the arrow next to *Type of Sign Up* to view your choices and select one.

2. Fill in the *Name of Your Group* section. Think of who's receiving this opportunity to sign up and name your group accordingly. I named my group "Mrs. Elliott's Fourth Grade."

3. SignUpGenius will remember all the groups you create. This is a handy feature because it means you won't have to type in the e-mail addresses each time you send out a sign-up.

4. You'll also need to fill in the *Title of Sign Up* section. I called mine "Parent Volunteers."

5. Last, you'll need to provide a *Description* of your sign-up. Type your message in the text box. Here's the place to provide parents with directions to understand the purpose of the sign-up. Click on the orange *Continue* button.

SELECT A THEME

1. Now here's the fun part: you get to be all cutesy. You can choose from all kinds of backgrounds and designs for your sign-up sheet.

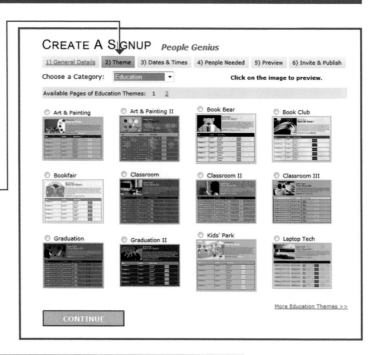

2. If you want to preview one of the templates, click on the page you're interested in. A bigger image of the page will pop up. Click on the bigger image to return back to all the choices.

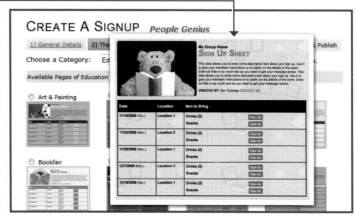

3. To see even more designs, look at the top of the screen where it says *Choose a Category* and click on the arrow next to the box to open a drop-down menu.

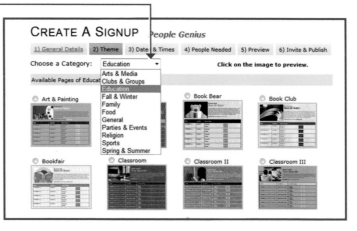

4. Once you've made up your mind, click on the little circle next to the image of the background you want to use. Then scroll to the bottom of the screen and click on the *Continue* button.

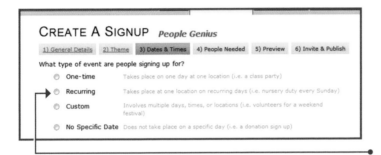

SELECT DATES & TIMES

1. Looking good. You should now see a screen that asks, "What type of event are people signing up for?" You're given four choices to select from. Click on the little circle next to the choice that matches your needs.

2. Depending on which type of event you've selected, a window will open requesting that you fill in information about your event's date and time.

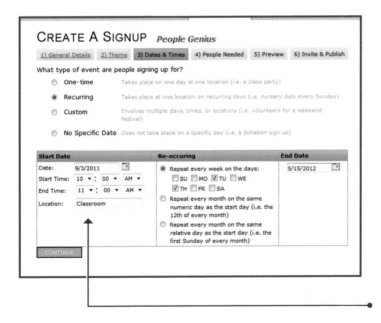

3. For example, here I selected a *Recurring* event. I filled out my form to request that volunteers come to my classroom each Tuesday and Thursday from 10 a.m. to 11 a.m. from September through May.

4. If you select *One-time* event, you'll have an RSVP option. Click on the RSVP box to reveal your options. You can have SignUpGenius send a reminder before your event. You can also decide if you want others to be able to see who has responded.

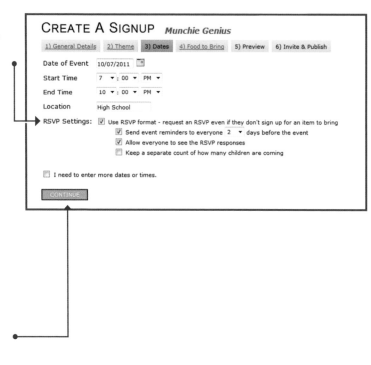

FILL IN THE DETAILS

1. After you've selected your type of event, filled in the dates and times, and clicked the orange *Continue* button, you'll be brought to a screen where you'll be asked to fill in more details about your needs for either people or items.

2. Continuing with my earlier example, this is where I can specify that I'd I like two parents to assist me for my math center time at 10 a.m. and two more parents to help me with my bulletin board at 10:30 a.m.

3. Since this is a recurring event, I have the option of showing all of those dates on the finished sign-up sheet or choosing selected dates and times.

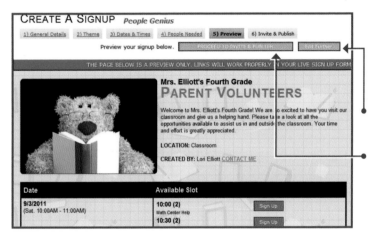

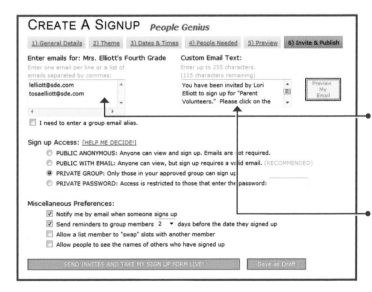

4. Notice that if you want the events or supplies listed alphabetically you can select that option using the drop-down menu next to *Sort the Sign Up Slots*. When you're done, click the orange *Update* button.

5. How cool is that? You should now see a preview of your sign-up. Isn't it great? If you want to make changes, look at the top of the screen and click on the orange *Edit Further* button. If you love it, click on the *Proceed to Invite & Publish* button.

INVITE & PUBLISH

1. You'll now be on the *Invite & Publish* page. At the top left-hand side of the page is a box titled *Enter Emails for*. This is where you type in the e-mail addresses for anyone you want to receive this sign-up.

2. To the right of that box is another box titled *Custom Email Text*. This is where you'll write the message you want to accompany the link to your sign-up.

3. You have four options for selecting who can view and actually sign up on your invite. Most likely you'll choose the *Private Group* option because it's designed for a small group of 30 or fewer, and you probably know everyone's e-mail address.

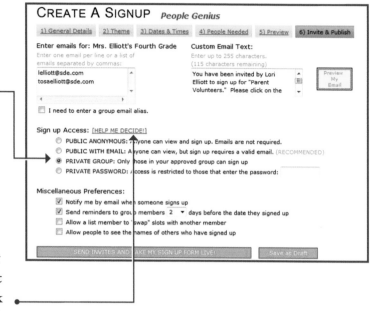

4. There may be a time, however, when you'd like to contact a larger group, or not enter e-mail addresses at all. To help you decide, look above the list of options and click on the *Help Me Decide* button.

MISCELLANEOUS PREFERENCES

1. You'll want to consider the options listed in the *Miscellaneous Preferences* section. I always select the first option that says *Notify Me by Email When Someone Signs Up.*

2. The second option about sending reminders is pretty handy. If you choose to have the site do it for you, you won't have to send reminders yourself. To preview the e-mail SignUpGenius will send, click on the yellow box that says *Preview My Email.*

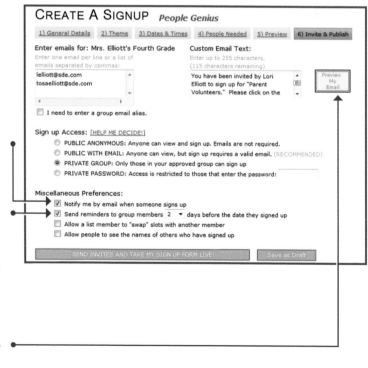

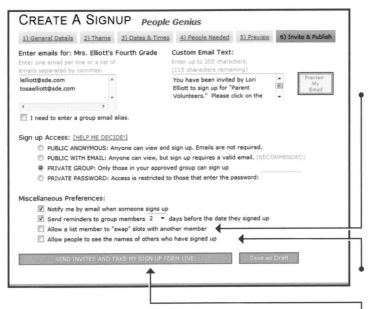

3. My personal preference is not to allow a parent to swap times or supplies with someone else, so I don't check the third box that allows members to swap slots.

4. I also don't want everyone to see who's bringing in what or when a parent is attending a parent-teacher conference. So I don't check that last box. This may not be true for your situation, but it's good to weigh your options here.

5. When you're happy with your selections and don't want to make further changes, click on *Send Invites and Take My Sign Up Form Live!*

6. A new screen will appear to tell you that your sign-up is complete.

7. Well done! SignUpGenius will now manage all the details. You can check your account to see the progress, or if you selected the option to be notified by e-mail when someone signs up, you should soon be receiving those e-mails.

Look What You Can Do

Now that you know how to use SignUp-Genius, think of all the things you can do. Let's think through a typical school year. To start the year, you may want parents to sign up to volunteer, read to students, share their experiences, or help you run off copies. Just as soon as you get everyone's e-mail address, send out a SignUpGenius form to see how many parents are willing to help out.

Next item on the to-do list is the monthly snack list. With just a few clicks, parents can sign up to bring snacks for the entire year. The beautiful part is that SignUpGenius will automatically send out the snack reminders for us. Sweet!

Moving right along: try using SignUpGenius when it's time for parent-teacher conferences, instead of playing paper or phone tag. Parents may be more apt to participate if the message comes directly to their computer or phone.

Time for a field trip? Need parent volunteers to ride the bus, manage groups of students, or protect the ice chest full of sack lunches? Put SignUpGenius to work yet again. What a relief to eliminate paper shuffling and the potential for lost papers.

A QUICK TIP

As the teacher, you can always sign people up yourself. For example, if a parent calls you, writes a note, or signs up using a printed sign-up sheet, as the administrator, you can sign them into the site (with or without their e-mail). That way you can keep track of everything in one spot.

Get Real

There's one obvious problem with the SignUpGenius solution. There may be parents without Internet access or e-mail addresses. It'll take a little investigating at the beginning of the school year, but find out what technology is available to parents outside of the classroom. An easy way to do this is with a question on the beginning-of-the-year enrollment form. Under the space where parents are asked to provide their e-mail address, include the options, "I do not have e-mail access" or "I do not want to be contacted by e-mail." Make sure to provide those parents with paper copies of the sign-up forms.

SOLUTION **3**

Post on Facebook

Facebook is everywhere. Sitting at your breakfast table you've probably seen wording such as "Like us on Facebook" on your favorite cereal box or yogurt container. What exactly does it mean to "Like" something on Facebook? Well, if you log in to Facebook, find a company's page, and click on "Like," then whenever the company wants to tempt you with a new product or if they have important information they'd like to share, they'll send out a message, and, since you "Like" them, you'll see that message on your Facebook Home page. More and more people rely on sites like Facebook to give them up-to-the-minute news and announcements.

Did you know that Facebook offers individuals the option to create an organization or group page, too? It functions much differently from what most people think of when they think about Facebook. When you create a special organization or group page just for your classroom, there's no need to "friend" anyone, plus there are several options you can choose from to set up your page so it can be as safe as possible.

Since so many parents are already on Facebook daily to check the status of their friends and family, don't you think it would make a lot of sense to put class information on such a popular and constantly used social media site? You could use your class page to keep parents updated about the learning and events going on in the classroom. Sound like a plan? Setting up your own class page is a really simple process. Take a look and see.

Let's Get Started

1. If you haven't already set up a Facebook account, now's the time to do it. Head over to http://www.facebook.com/. The very first page you see is the registration page.

2. Fill in your name, e-mail address, and password. You do have to provide your birthday, and that's a safety measure so students under the age of 13 don't try to set up an account. After filling in all of the information, click on the green *Sign Up* button.

3. If you already have a Facebook page, then you don't need to register again. Instead, just log in to your account.

4. Once you're logged in to your account, look at the top left-hand side of your screen. You should see your name.

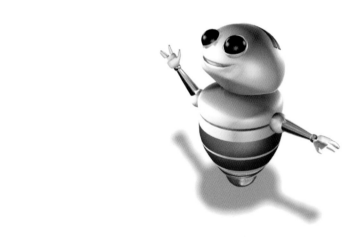

5. Now, you're going to type in the web address you need to create your organization or group page. So go ahead and type in http://www.facebook.com/pages/create.php/.

NAME YOUR PAGE

1. You should see a page with six boxes, each with its own icon. You want to click on the middle one in the top row that says *Company, Organization, or Institution*.

2. Doing okay? When you click on the box, a *Choose a Category* option and *Company Name* section will pop up.

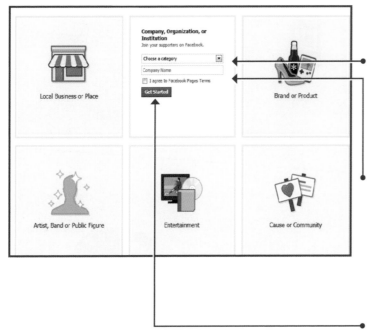

3. Pull down the arrow next to the *Choose a Category* option and select *Education.* *Company Name* is where you get to name your class page. Try to name it something parents will remember: "Dr. Elliott's Updates," for instance.

4. You'll need to accept Facebook's terms by clicking on the box below *Company Name.* To read the terms, click on the blue text. If you agree, click on the blue *Get Started* button.

ADD A PICTURE FROM YOUR COMPUTER

1. Say cheese! This is the section where you set up your profile for your class page. Consider loading an image that parents will associate with your class. Maybe it's your picture, a picture of the classroom, or a class mascot, etc.

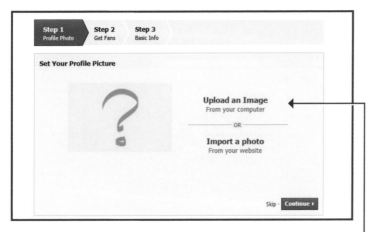

2. First, make sure you have the picture you want to use saved somewhere on your computer. Click on *Upload an Image from your Computer.*

3. A pop-up window will open asking you to select an image file from your computer. Click on *Browse*.

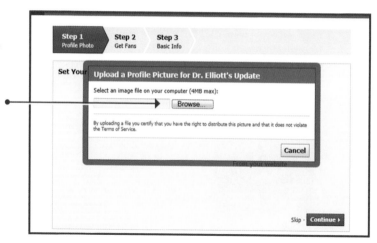

4. Your computer will show you all of the places where you can look for your picture. For example, I save my photos in my *Pictures* library.

5. Within my *Pictures* library, I organize photos into separate folders, usually by date or project. The photo I want to use is in a folder named "bookimages2." So I'd click on that folder to open it, and then I'd click on the photo to select it.

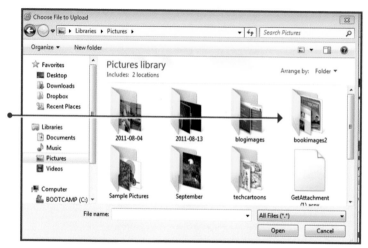

6. After you've found and selected your photo, click on the *Open* button.

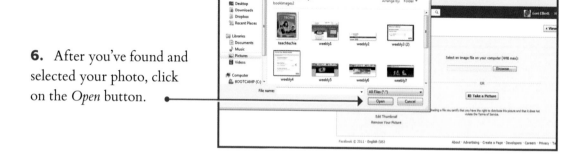

7. Excellent. Now you should see your picture on the computer screen. If you like it, click on *Continue*. Not really what you want to use? Click on *Upload an Image* again and find another picture you like better.

GET THE WORD OUT

1. Step 1 is done; now let's move on to Step 2 in the process. If you're familiar with Facebook, then the wording here will be familiar.

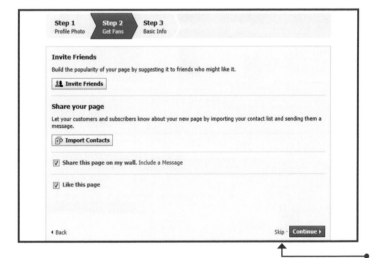

2. If you want to notify others you're already friends with on Facebook about your new class page, you can. If this doesn't interest you, or you aren't really comfortable with Facebook yet, ignore this section and click *Skip*.

3. In Step 3, you'll be asked if you want to share your website and if you'd like to provide a short blurb describing your class page.

4. If you have a classroom website or blog, I think it would be a great idea to link it here so that as parents check out your class page on Facebook, they can also wander over to your classroom website.

5. The *About* blurb should make the purpose of your class page very clear. Let parents know that you'll be using it to share classroom updates and information. Click *Continue* and let's keep going.

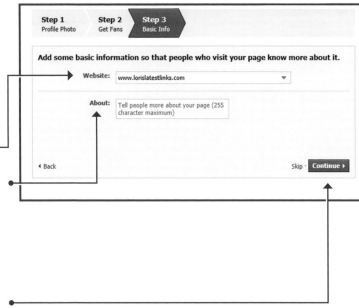

POST A MESSAGE

1. Hooray! How about that? You should see your new class page staring right at you. This is the *Get Started* page that Facebook provides.

2. Go ahead and post a message. Find *Option 3, Post Status Updates* and click on the gray *Post Update* button.

3. The screen will change and show a text box at the top of the page. Go ahead and type in your first message to your students' parents. Click on the blue *Share* button to publish your message.

SELECT YOUR SETTINGS

1. It looks great doesn't it? Now let's do a little behind-the-scenes work. You don't have to do all the steps I'm about to mention, but I do encourage you to spend a little time tightening up the permissions.

2. Notice at the top right-hand side of your page the *Admins . . . See All* bar. Click on *See All*. This opens a page that allows you to access some important settings for your Facebook class page account.

3. Look at the left-hand side of the screen. Click on *Your Settings*.

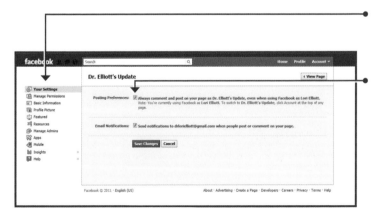

4. I recommend that you keep the *Posting Preferences* option selected. That way you'll be able to post updates to your class page even if you're logged on to your personal account without your updates ending up on your personal page.

5. Next, if you want to receive an e-mail when someone comments on your page, keep the *Email Notifications* box selected, too. Otherwise, just click on the box and deselect it. Click on *Save Changes* after making those two decisions.

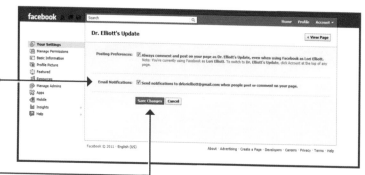

MANAGE FACEBOOK PERMISSIONS

1. Look again at the choices in the column on the left-hand side of the page. Click on *Manage Permissions*.

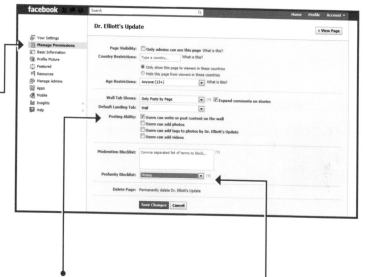

2. The choices listed in the top section are fairly standard. The things you'll want to be concerned about are listed in the second and third sections of this window.

3. Take a look at the *Posting Ability* options. What do you want users of this page to be allowed to do? If you'd like to allow parents to write or post comments on your wall, leave the box checked, otherwise remove the checkmark by clicking on it.

4. Since I use this for education, I don't want others to tag pictures with me in them on this page or add photos or video. I check each of those boxes in order to deselect them.

5. The other thing I want tight control over is language. If you do allow parents to post comments, be sure to change the *Profanity Blocklist* in the last section of this window from *None* to *Strong* in order to filter content.

6. Click on *Save Changes* when you've made all of your choices.

POST SOME MORE

1. To get back to your class page, go to the top right-hand side and click on *View Page*.

2. You'll be back at your class page. Look around the text box. By clicking on the words written in blue, you can share *Status*, *Photos*, *Links*, *Videos*, or even ask a *Question*.

3. Use the *Link* option to share helpful resources for students to use at home for review, enrichment, or homework. Copy the website address and then paste it in the box provided when you click on *Link*.

4. The *Question* feature is a good one because it can be used to get students involved. Post a question related to something you're learning in class. Ask parents to post feedback from their child to answer the question.

5. For example, if you're learning about spiders, you could post, "Are spiders insects, arachnids, or mammals?" Use the feedback you receive to kick off your lesson the next day.

GET THE WORD OUT & KEEP ON POSTIN'

1. Whew! Now that you have all of that accomplished, what happens when you log out of Facebook or close down your computer?

2. The next time you log in to your Facebook account, you'll see your new page listed under *Pages* on the left-hand side of your Home page. To post new messages to your page, click on the name of your page and you're good to go.

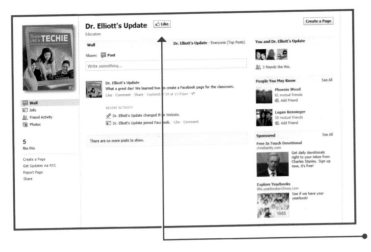

3. Be sure to get the word out about your class page. Use all of your other forms of classroom communication (newsletters, e-mails, websites, etc.) to share the name of your Facebook page with parents.

4. Ask parents to log in to Facebook, search for your site, and then click on the *Like* button found next to your page's name so they'll get your updates. Way to go you social-media maniac!

Look What You Can Do

Are you still not sure exactly how you'll use your new class page? Think of all the things you usually put in a newsletter or ask your students to remind their parents. I used to write about things such as upcoming test dates, library book due-date reminders, changes to the Friday lunch menu, etc. on the board. The problem was, once students walked or ran out the door, they usually forgot everything. It's so nice to be able to quickly post those reminders on the Facebook page and rest assured that most of the parents will get the note before their child even arrives back home!

Get yourself in the routine of using your Facebook class page. Every time you're about to jot yourself a note to tell students or parents something, post it instead it to your Facebook class page. Create a sense of anticipation among parents by posting valuable, novel, and helpful updates. Parents will really appreciate the constant communication you are providing.

Get Real

Now that I've made Facebook sound all rosy, let me approach the thorns. Even though many educators see social networking as a viable and effective tool in communicating with parents and students, many lawmakers, school boards, and administrators disagree. There's a very big difference between using Facebook in a personal way to friend parents and students and using it in a professional manner to inform. Please check your district policy regarding social networking. It's a sticky subject in many states.

Guard your class page against improper use. If you do choose to set up a class page, make sure parents and administrators understand how you plan to use it and make your expectations clear. Set up tight security restrictions so inappropriate or uncomfortable things are not shared with the whole world. Revisit pages 96–98 for specific ways to safeguard your page.

A QUICK TIP

Use your mobile phone wherever you are to update your page. Go to the *Get Started* screen for your class page. Use Option 4 to set up your class page to accept either e-mail or texts from your mobile phone. Then when you think of something in the middle of your son's soccer game, you can grab your phone, take care of business, and get back to cheering!

Publish Newsletters with MailChimp

In addition to being a teacher, I'm also the mom of two spectacular kids, and I have a confession to make. Over the years I have, on occasion, dropped the ball and missed some important news from their teachers. There have been Fridays when I forgot to see what was lurking in those backpacks, followed by chaotic Monday mornings when we were already running late and one of my kids would casually mention, "Mom, I'm supposed to bring in snacks for the whole class today. It's our week." Are you kidding me? There's not a granola bar, pretzel, or fishy cracker to be found in the house. If I had only read the newsletters over the weekend!

As teachers we work hard and put in a lot of effort to create eye-catching documents, but how can we ensure that they make it home or that our audience gets a chance to read them? Instead of filling backpacks with paper copies, why not send newsletters via e-mail? Most parents have an e-mail account for work or personal use and check them several times a day. Okay, be honest, are you imagining a dull-looking e-mail with no fun graphics? Then let me introduce you to MailChimp. Interesting name, huh? Well, there's no monkeying around here. MailChimp is a free online tool that'll help you create flashy-looking digital newsletters that you can e-mail to everyone on your contact list. Your students' families will be so impressed by the e-mails. You'll look like an accomplished graphic artist. More importantly, your information and updates will be viewed by a greater percentage of parents.

Let's Get Started

MailChimp is used most often by the business world for marketing. As we start working through the process, you'll notice that I'll ignore lots of things in the program and that's because our purpose is to inform parents, not sell a product to thousands of consumers. I'm going to take you through the easiest steps possible to get your newsletters written and e-mailed out as quickly as you can.

GATHER E-MAIL ADDRESSES

1. You'll need the e-mail addresses of the parents, and any other people, you want to send your newsletter to. You'll also need their permission to send them e-mail messages using MailChimp.

2. I like to request this type of information in my back-to-school class information packet. If some people would rather not receive these e-mails, or don't have access to e-mail, don't include them in the list. Instead provide them with a paper copy of the newsletter.

3. Let parents know that MailChimp won't sell their e-mail address to another list or use it to send them spam. Also, when you send out a newsletter via MailChimp, the recipients aren't able to see the e-mail addresses of the other recipients.

OPEN AN ACCOUNT

1. The first step is to go to http://mailchimp.com/. This is the opening screen. Click on the *Sign Up Free* button to get started.

2. On the next screen, notice the little message under the words "The Forever Free Plan." MailChimp is free as long as you don't send over 12,000 e-mails a month. Think that's doable? It works for me.

3. If you feel the same way, just fill in your e-mail, username, and password. Click on *Create My Account* when you have those things completed.

4. After completing the account information, you'll see a screen that tells you to check your e-mail to activate the account.

5. Go ahead and check your e-mail. MailChimp will have sent you a message containing a link. Click on the link. That will activate your account and take you back to MailChimp.

6. There's just one more security measure. MailChimp provides two words that you must type in. Get your glasses on and decode that scribble text. Type in the words and then click on *Confirm Signup* to finish the activation process.

7. Ready? Next MailChimp will ask you to fill out your contact information. You need to fill in your e-mail address, name, address, organization, website, and security question.

8. For address, use your school's address. If you have a classroom website, include it; otherwise just fill in your school's site.

9. For the *Organization* field, I recommend you fill in what you'd like to call your newsletter because the site automatically places the organization name on the main header of your newsletter. In my example, I filled in, "Dr. Elliott's Class."

10. When you have completed the form, click on the blue *Save and Get Started* button.

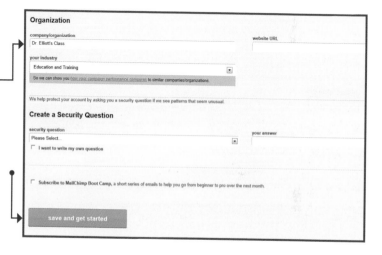

SET UP YOUR MAILING LIST

1. You should now see what's called the *Dashboard* screen. The first step is to create a subscriber list. This is the list of all the people to whom you want to send your newsletter. Under Step 1, click on the *Create a Subscriber List* button.

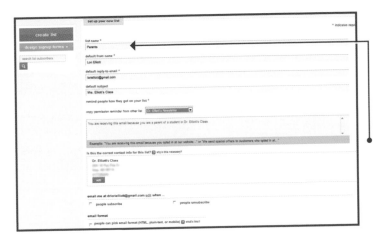

2. Here you'll be asked to type in a list name. In other words, what do you want to call this group of people to whom you'll be sending your newsletter? I typed in "Parents."

3. On the next few entries, don't let the term "default" throw you. Just fill in your name, school e-mail address, and a subject line.

4. You'll also type a very short message to let readers know why they're receiving this e-mail message from you. I wrote that they were receiving it because they're parents of students in my class.

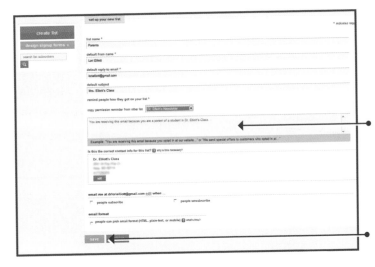

5. When you're done, go to the bottom of the page and click on the blue *Save* button.

ADD NAMES TO YOUR LIST

1. Your list is now created. Next you need to enter the parents' e-mail addresses to your list.

2. If you don't have too many e-mail addresses to work with and because they're probably not saved on a spreadsheet, you're going to have to enter them manually. Look at the choices written in red under your list name and click on *Add People*.

3. Type in the e-mail address and the full name of the first person on your list, and then click on the box at the bottom of the page to indicate that this person has given you permission to send this e-mail. Next, click on the blue *Subscribe* button.

4. A screen will appear showing the information you entered for the person you added to the list. It's not necessary to complete the social data for each of your e-mail recipients.

5. To add the next e-mail address, look to the top of the screen and click on the gray *Add People* button. Continue this process until you have entered all of the e-mail addresses to your list.

SET UP YOUR NEWSLETTER

1. You've finished the hard part. You won't have to type those addresses in again. MailChimp will store your list and whenever you want to send something to that group of people, you'll simply need to select that list.

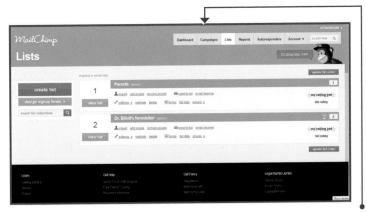

2. Now, look at the top of the page where you are. You'll see a blue band containing the options, *Dashboard, Campaigns, Lists, Reports, AutoResponders*, and *Account*. Click on *Campaigns*.

3. In MailChimp a newsletter is called a *Campaign*. Don't let that wording throw you. Look at the left-hand side of the screen and locate the red *Create Campaign* button.

4. Roll your mouse over the *Create Campaign* button to activate a drop-down menu. You'll see four choices. Click on *Regular ol' Campaign*. This is the basic, most commonly used newsletter option.

5. If you have more than one list created, MailChimp will ask you to select which list you want to send this newsletter to.

6. Let's say you created one list for parents and another one for teachers. To select your parent list, click on the circle next to *Parents*. Now, look to the right-hand side of your list and click on the blue *Send to Entire List* button.

7. Don't be alarmed with all of the choices on the next screen. You're going to stay on the left-hand side of the page. Name the campaign. Remember this is just the name of your newsletter.

8. You'll also type in a message subject, your name, and the e-mail address that you want parents to use if they want to contact you. Ignore everything else. Click on *Next* to continue.

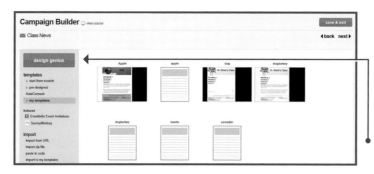

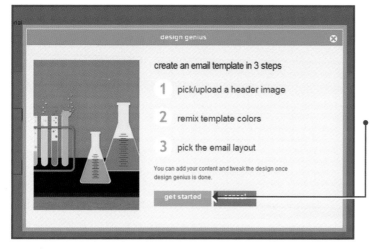

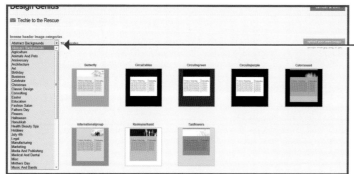

CHOOSE A TEMPLATE

1. Now for the creative part. You get to design and write your newsletter. Look at the left-hand side of the screen and click on the red *Design Genius* button. This will give you plenty of options for creating your newsletter.

2. A pop-up window labeled *Design Genius* will open. Click on the blue *Get Started* button.

3. Here you can choose a background for your newsletter. Notice at the top left-hand side of the screen a box titled *Browse Header Image Categories*. Click on the arrow to activate a drop-down menu with many more background category choices.

4. Select the background you want to use by clicking on its image.

5. Once you click on the background image, the next page will show you a preview. The title is based on the organization name you entered when you set up the campaign.

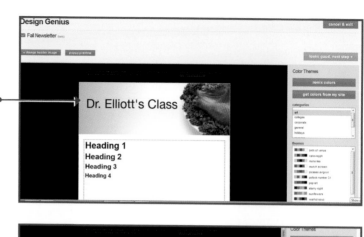

6. If you want to change the title, roll your mouse over the text and a pop-up menu will appear. Click on *Design Header*. You can also delete the template text and type in your own words on the rest of the page.

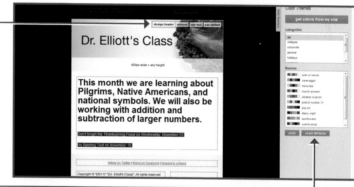

7. On the right-hand side are all the options for changing the colors and fonts. Have fun playing here or just click on *Looks Good, Next Step* if you like the background just the way it is.

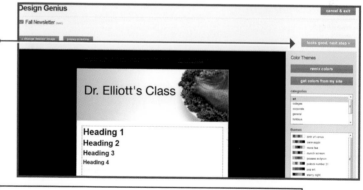

8. On the right-hand side of the screen you'll see layout options for your newsletter. Click on the layout that you like best, and then click on the blue *Save & Add Content* button.

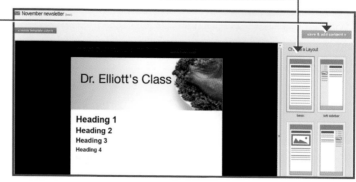

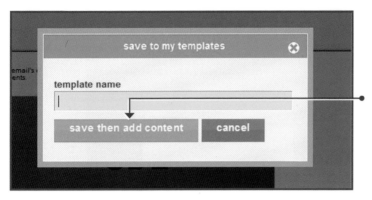

9. A pop-up window will appear and ask you to name the template. Type in a name and then click on the *Save Then Add Content* button.

WRITE YOUR NEWSLETTER

1. Now it's time to write your newsletter. Click on any box in the template to edit it. Highlight and delete those unwanted words and fill in your information.

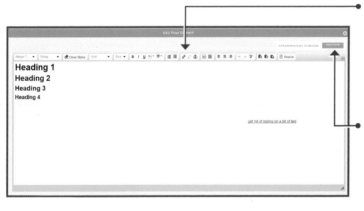

2. Look at the toolbar across the top of the text box. You'll find that it's very similar to word processing programs that you're already familiar with. Click on *Save Now* to preview your work as you're typing.

3. Just a note here. At the very top of the template, written in tiny print, is a message about using a box to offer a short e-mail teaser.

4. You'll want to delete this message and replace it with your own text or delete it all together. Otherwise it appears on the finished newsletter. Not good.

5. When you finish editing your newsletter and are ready to send it, click on *Next*.

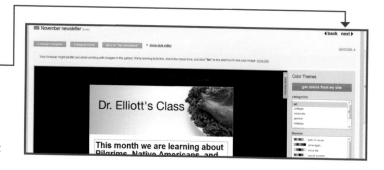

MAIL YOUR NEWSLETTER

1. Now you'll be staring at a screen with lots of codes and confusing-looking things. Do not be alarmed. This is the technical side of the message. No worries.

2. The one thing I'd have you click on here is the gray *Copy Text from HTML* button. This just makes sure that the reader will be able to view your message. Click on *Next* again.

3. You're almost there. You'll see a page full of yellow sections with your information. Here you can double-check things once again before you send this puppy out.

4. To send out the newsletter scroll all the way to the bottom of the page and click on the red *Send Now* button.

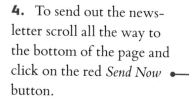

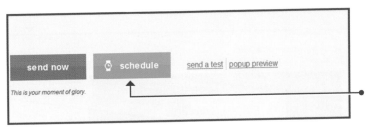

5. If you'd rather set a time and date to have MailChimp send the newsletter out later, click on the blue *Schedule* button. This is a great feature for those of us who don't like to procrastinate.

6. If you clicked on *Send Now*, a confirmation message will pop up asking you if you're sure that you want to continue. Click on *Send Campaign*.

7. High fives! Parents will think you're so tech savvy and on top of your game. I know I'm impressed!

8. If you clicked on *Schedule*, you'll be asked to select your time zone and set a delivery date and time. Once you've done that, click on the red *Schedule* button.

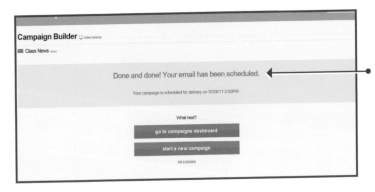

9. Your work here is, as they say, done and done!

Look What You Can Do

You can make your newsletter look really great by adding class photos. To do this, open the draft of the campaign you want to use. Roll your mouse over the section of the template where you want to add a photo. An *Edit* button will appear; click on it. Depending on which section of the template you've selected, you'll either be brought right to an *Upload Picture* screen, or you may see a toolbar. If you see the toolbar, click on the icon that looks like a *Picture* to get to the *Upload Picture* screen. After you've found and selected your photo, click on the *Open* button. You now have a newsletter with a totally customized look.

Get Real

Some parents may not have access to e-mail or choose not to participate in receiving class e-mails; you'll need to provide those people with a paper copy instead. Add yourself to the MailChimp list and print your copy of the newsletter to send home with those not participating online.

A QUICK TIP

Check to see how many parents have viewed your newsletter and add new people to your e-mail lists from your mobile device. You can access the iPhone app from the Apple App Store. The Blackberry app can be found at http://minichimp.com/, and the Android version is available at Android Market.

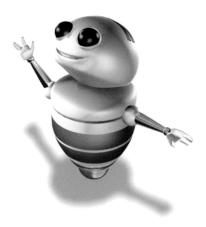

Reenergize Your Instruction

Building Your Store of Professional Resources

I honestly believe that teaching is the most rewarding calling in the world, but it can also be the most challenging. As professionals, we have so many demands on our time. Let's put aside the time we spend each day in the classroom with 25 or so unique individuals, each with his own interests, learning styles, and needs. We also take our duties with us outside the classroom. We write newsletters and have conferences to communicate with parents; we work hard to create effective lessons; we attend staff meetings; and we engage in professional development.

Quality, ongoing training is what most of us desire. Don't you love that invigorated and excited feeling you get when you learn something useful at a workshop. Even though you may have secretly looked forward to a day away from your classroom (a whole day when you can sit down, sip your coffee leisurely, and go to the bathroom whenever you want), isn't it amazing how eager you are to get back to your students the next day to try out those new ideas? And don't you love it when you're at a conference and you connect with another teacher who shares the same interests you do. Meeting new colleagues is a terrific bonus feature of professional development.

We want to do the best for our students, but finding the time and money to continually develop ourselves as professionals can be tough.

Most districts will never be able to provide training to fit the needs of each teacher. In many instances, we have to be independent and seek out our own learning.

Is Technology the Answer?

Using technology is the easiest way to find resources to fit your interests. Instead of actually going off-site for a meeting, you can join a webinar. You no longer must travel to the local university for graduate courses; you can take them online. While those two options certainly give you more flexibility, they aren't always free. For free, there are thousands of online sites for educators, but how do you find the good ones? I mean honestly, how many times has this scenario happened to you? You want to find a writing lesson to really wow your students. It seems like a simple task. You head to the computer and start searching for ideas on Google. The more you search, the more anxious you become. You click on dozens of links, and nothing seems to hit the mark. How is it with all the information on the World Wide Web, you can't find a single writing lesson to excite your third graders?

Work Smarter, Not Harder

It's true. There are amazing classroom resources available to you just a click away, and it's possible to continue to develop yourself as a professional using online resources and tools. You just need to know where to look. In this chapter, I'd like to introduce you to some of my favorite resources for teachers. I'll show you how to develop a Personal Learning Network (PLN) with Twitter, and I'll show you how to create your own one-stop personalized professional development site using Google Reader.

As for finding good lessons online, you'll hit a home run every time with a site called Read Write Think. Here you'll not only find quality literacy lessons, but also ideas for using many free, interactive tools with students. Plus there's a whole section of articles and news that focuses on professional development.

Finally, I'll share an online tool that will save you oodles of time and frustration. If you've ever tried to create a rubric, then you'll love RubiStar. With the rubrics you generate using this tool, it'll look as if you've attended a workshop focused on creating them. So go ahead and grab yourself a cup of coffee to enjoy as you embark on your own independent journey into the world of online professional development.

Network on Twitter

Tweet has a new meaning. It used to be what a bird did on a warm, spring day. Now it's what millions of people do daily to express their thoughts or share information. On Twitter you Tweet. A Tweet is a message of up to 140 characters long that you send to anyone who follows you. If you follow someone on Twitter, it means you've signed up to receive that person's messages. Whenever the person sends a Tweet, it'll appear on your Twitter home page. Twitter is a social networking site that connects people with similar interests.

Most people think of celebrities when they think of Twitter. It's been reported that certain stars like Ellen and Ashton have more followers than the population of some countries. Do you really need to know what Lady Gaga is doing moment-by-moment? I think not.

Twitter has become one of the most commonly used communication tools for teachers today. It's true. Thousands of educators, myself included, are using Twitter to create their own Personal Learning Networks. A Personal Learning Network (PLN) uses social media to establish a group of people who share ideas and learn from each other. On Twitter, you don't only stay connected with teachers you know; you meet new colleagues and connect with leaders in education. You can choose to follow authors you admire and others who can help you to grow as a professional. The key to Twitter is who you choose to follow.

So, what have I personally gained from being on Twitter? First, I stay ahead of the curve with new resources, teaching ideas, and policies. When people share a web tool they like, I check it out. I'd probably never have found certain websites without the help of Twitter. Second, I've found opportunities for grants and contests. Grant money can be tough to find these days, but Twitter keeps me hopping with possibilities. Finally, I can keep up with trends in education. For example, when the movie *Waiting for Superman* was released, the backlash against the perceived negative perspective on education was all over Twitter. Teachers banded together for improvements and changes in schools because so many of them were outraged.

Let's Get Started

Twitter is actually pretty powerful. It gets the message out before most other forms of media. I came across this wonderful anonymous quote recently, "Facebook is where you find the people you know; Twitter is where you find the people you should know." Finding people you should know is a simple process and I'm happy to guide you through it.

SET UP AN ACCOUNT

1. Head to http://twitter.com/ to set up your Twitter account. To join Twitter you'll need to provide your full name, e-mail address, and a password. When you've completed the information, click on the yellow *Sign Up* button.

2. The next screen shows you the information you provided. If there's a problem with something you entered, you can correct it here. This is also where you can choose to accept a username Twitter suggests or create one of your own.

3. When all the information is complete, make sure to read the *Terms of Service* posted on the page. If you agree to the terms, then click on the *Create My Account* button.

4. Now you have your Twitter account ready to go. The new window that appears is the welcome page. Here you'll see an example of a Tweet. Click on the blue *Next* button to continue the set-up process.

FIND PEOPLE YOU WANT TO KNOW

1. Twitter offers a list of suggested people to Follow. If you happen to be interested in receiving Tweets from these people, click on the *Follow* button next to a name. Otherwise just click on *Skip this Step* at the bottom of the page.

2. Next, you'll see a page of popular people and brands. You can click on a category to search for brands or people related to your interests. You can also type in a topic that interests you in the search bar at the top right-hand corner of the screen.

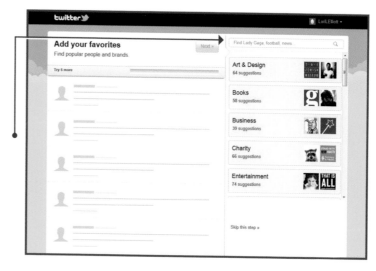

3. Go ahead and type the word "education" in the search bar. Scroll through to see all of your options. When you find an organization or individual that you're interested in following, click on the *Follow* button.

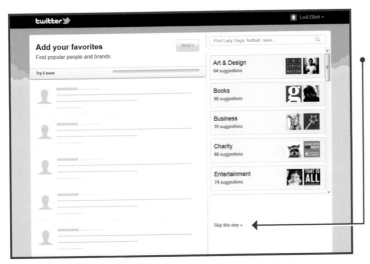

4. If you'd rather not search for "education" just yet, click on *Skip this Step* at the bottom of the page.

5. There are other ways to find educators on Twitter, which I'll discuss later in this chapter.

FIND PEOPLE YOU ALREADY KNOW

1. The final step in the set-up process is to look in your e-mail contacts for people you might want to follow.

2. You can search your various accounts like Gmail, Yahoo, Hotmail, and others to locate people you know who are also on Twitter.

3. If you want to try this, click on the *Search Contacts* button next to the service you use. A list of your contacts who are also on Twitter will show. You just need to click on *Follow* next to an individual's name.

4. If you want to Follow everyone in your e-mail contacts, look to the top of the screen and click on the button that says *Follow All*.

5. If you don't use any of these e-mail providers, you can find friends just by using the *Search* option.

6. For example, to follow me you would go to the search box at the top of the screen and type in "drloriel-liott." This will take you to my page and if you want to follow me, then you click on *Follow* next to my name.

7. If you're not interested in this process, go to the bottom of the page and click on *Skip this Step*.

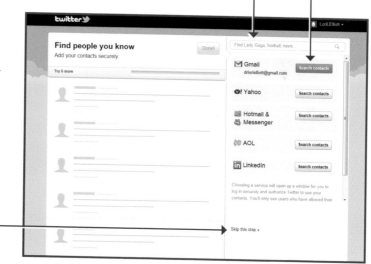

SET UP YOUR PROFILE

1. You're now on the *Get Started on Twitter* page. Even if you haven't followed a single person yet, you're ready to set up your Twitter page.

2. It's important to set up your Profile so others can find you based on your interests and recognize you based on the picture you post.

3. Look on the right-hand side of the page. Find Option 3: *Set Up Your Pro-file*. If you'd like to upload a photo of yourself or an image of something that you like, click on *Upload a Profile Picture*.

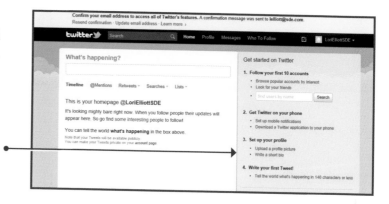

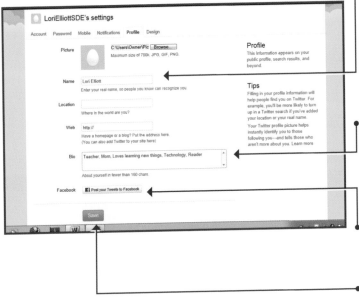

4. When the next page loads, click on the gray *Browse* button.

5. You'll see a pop-up window showing your computer's documents. Locate where you have stored the image you want to use. Select the image by clicking on it, and then click on *Open*.

6. Your name should already be filled in. You can type in your location and website or blog address if you want to make those known. If not, leave them empty.

7. The *Bio* section is important. This is what is placed on your profile; it provides the terms people might use while searching Twitter. So, use words that describe you professionally. I filled in words such as teacher, Mom, technology, and reader.

8. The last option is about Facebook. If you want your Tweets to also be posted on your Facebook account, you can click this option. Once you're finished with all your choices, click *Save* at the bottom of the screen.

9. Next, let's customize your Twitter page. Look to the top of the page and click on the *Design* tab.

10. The *Design* tab is where you can select another theme, or background, if you want your Twitter page to have a different look. Click on *Save Changes* when you're finished.

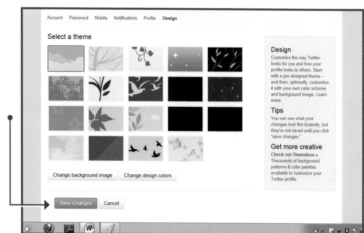

TWEET! TWEET!

1. You should now be on your home page. There will be a message here from Twitter explaining this. Now, you can start Tweeting.

2. Look to the right side of the page to Option 4, *Write Your First Tweet*. Click on the text that says *Tell the world what's happening in 140 characters or less*.

3. You'll then see the pop-up window waiting for you to type your first Tweet.

4. Type in your message or thought. Notice as you type there is a number countdown so you know when you're reaching the 140-character mark. Click on *Tweet* when you're finished.

5. You'll now see your home page the way it will look from now on. Each time you or anyone you follow posts a Tweet, it'll show up here on the home page. You can also Tweet by clicking on the *What's Happening* box at the top of the page.

LOOK WHAT YOU'VE DONE

1. Now that I've shown you how to set up a new Twitter account, let me show you my real one. This is what Twitter looks like when you start to follow others.

2. Notice across the very top of the page you can choose *Home, Profile, Messages,* and *Who To Follow. Profile* will show you what you've posted.

3. *Messages* functions like e-mail. You can send or receive private messages from others here.

WHO TO FOLLOW

1. The last thing I want to talk about here is how to find educators to follow. Remember to click on the *Twitter* icons or *Follow Me* buttons you see on websites or blogs when you find a group or person that you'd like to hear more from.

2. I also suggest that you check to see who the people you follow like to follow and click on the *Follow* buttons of the indiviuals that interest you.

3. To do this click on a person's name whom you follow. When you get to that person's Twitter page, click on *Following*. Now browse through the list of names to see if there is someone you would like to learn more from, too.

4. Another great resource was created by teacher Gina Hartman to help other educators connect on Twitter. She uses a wiki called Twitter-4Teachers to organize the lists of teachers.

5. A wiki is a website that allows users to make changes and contributions. Find her wiki at http://twitter4teachers.pbworks.com/w/page/22554534/FrontPage/.

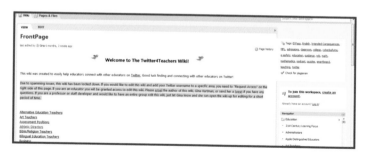

6. Look on the front page of the wiki. Click on the category that best describes you. You'll be shown the list of teachers. Click on the link provided to see a teacher's Twitter page. If you want to follow that teacher, then click the *Follow* button.

7. To add your name to the wiki, follow the directions on the front page or e-mail the author directly.

Look What You Can Do

I hope I've convinced you to build your own PLN using Twitter. Take part in Twitter discussions as well as read what others have to say. I've never met most of the people I follow on Twitter, but I feel like I know them very well because we share conversations on Twitter. If someone asks for help with something, reply. If teachers are all meeting on Twitter at a certain time for a certain topic, show up and share. Be an active Tweeter. Don't be timid about putting your ideas and questions out there. This is the place to connect with lots of people with simple 140-character messages.

A QUICK TIP

Tweet on the go! You probably don't go anywhere without your cell phone, so why not use it to make the most of Twitter. Use Twitter with text messaging. The only cost is your regular message and data rates. Visit https://twitter.com/devices/. Think of how easy it will be to Tweet when you think of something, even if you don't have WiFi.

Get Real

Most schools block Twitter because it's a social media site. You may have to access your account from home or on your cell phone. You can download a Twitter app on most smart phones for no charge. Visit https://twitter.com/#!/download/ for mobile app downloads.

Do understand that Twitter will only be effective if you choose to follow people who have something to say, and if you check your Tweets regularly.

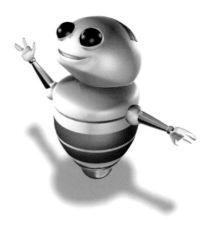

Stay Current Using Google Reader

I love to share my favorite technology resources with other teachers. I guess that's the reason I wrote this book and travel the country to talk with teachers. The one question I'm asked all the time is, "How do you know about this stuff?" I didn't start out as a techie; that happened by accident. I learned about most of this stuff the old fashioned way. I read about it. I read everything I can get my hands on, and the majority of the information I read these days comes from blogs and websites.

Reading blogs and websites is more than just a pastime for me. It's one of the most powerful professional development opportunities I can take advantage of daily. I don't always have lots of time to sit in meetings, attend workshops, or go to conferences. But I do usually have a few minutes here and there to skim the latest articles and posts between checking my e-mail and Facebook accounts.

But instead of wasting time repeatedly checking my favorite blogs and websites for updates, I use a tool called Google Reader, which allows you to read all of your favorite online sites in one place. At a glance, you can see which of your go-to blogs and websites has been updated, and you can decide if you want to read them now or later. It's kind of like creating your own digital magazine because you get to choose the resources you enjoy and read the articles that you're most interested in. With Google Reader you can create a personalized one-stop professional development site. You'll be surprised at how easy it is to set up and use.

Let's Get Started

Google Reader is a product offered by Google. It's free, but you'll need to set up an account first. Just having a Gmail account doesn't necessarily mean you have a Google account. I'll walk you through how to set up an account. If you already have one because you use Blogger or you've set up an account previously, then you should be able to log right in and get started.

SET UP YOUR ACCOUNT

1. Go to http://www. google.com/reader/. If you already have a Google account, then log in with your e-mail and password. If you need to set up an account, I'll help you do that now.

2. Notice the text in the in the top right-hand corner that says *Sign Up for a New Google Account.* Click on those words.

3. To register, you'll need to type in an e-mail address, password, location, your birthday, and word verification. The word verification is to make sure you're not a computer trying to set up an account.

4. Below the *Word Verification* you'll see Google Reader's *Terms of Service.* Take a moment to read the terms. If you agree, click on the *I Accept. Create My Account* button at the bottom of the page.

5. You should now be on the Google Reader page. Your screen is probably already filled with posts from some sites you may have no interest in at all. These sites are recommendations from Google.

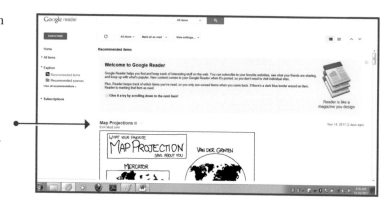

6. Let's get them out of the way so you can start building your own list of favorites.

ADD A SUBSCRIPTION

1. Look at the left-hand side of the screen. Find and click on the words *All Items* to remove the recommendations. Your screen will now say, "Your reading list is empty."

2. Now you can start adding your own subscriptions. A subscription is the website or blog you want to include on your page.

3. Look at the left-hand side of the screen again. This time click on the big red *Subscribe* button.

4. A pop-up window will open. This is where you type or paste in the website or blog address you'd like listed in your Google Reader. In the example, I typed in my blog address, www.lorislatestlinks.com. After you enter the address you want, click on the *Add* button.

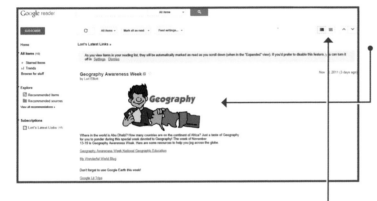

5. You'll see entries or articles from that site appear in the middle of the page.

VIEW YOUR SUBSCRIPTIONS

1. You can choose to view the entries or articles as a list or in expanded view. The expanded view allows you to see the highlights from the new entries.

2. To change from list view to expanded view, or vice versa, look to the top right-hand side of the screen. There are two icons.

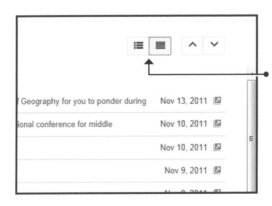

3. The first one resembles a *Bulleted List* and is the expanded view option. The second icon is the *List View* option. Click on either icon. That was pretty easy, right?

4. For each additional site you want to add to your Google Reader, simply click on the red *Subscribe* button, type in the address of the website or blog, and then click on the *Add* button.

5. Look at the left-hand side of the screen under the heading *Subscriptions*. Each time you add a new site, you'll also see it listed there.

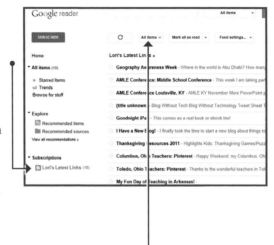

6. You can access each website or blog individually from the *Subscriptions* section by clicking on the one you want to read. Or, to view the most recent entries from all of your subscriptions in chronological order, click on *All Items*.

STAR AN ARTICLE OR POST

1. When you have the expanded view selected, you're able to do several things with each posting.

2. You can star an article or new post to read later. This is the digital equivalent of folding down the corner of a page in your magazine. Look to the bottom of the expanded box and click on the *Star* icon.

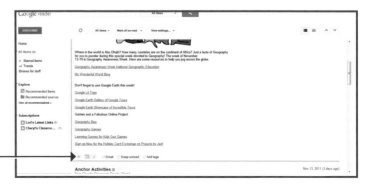

3. Now when you go back to List view you'll be able to see the star, which will remind you to read the information when it's convenient.

4. If you have several items that you've marked with stars, you don't have to scroll through the list to find them. Look at the left-hand side of the screen under the heading *All Items*.

5. Click on the *Starred Items* option. Now you can view a list of just your starred items. Pretty snazzy feature.

ORGANIZE YOUR SUBSCRIPTIONS

1. Once you have added several subscriptions to your page, you may want to create folders to organize them by theme or topic.

2. To do this, look below the *Subscriptions* heading and find the websites you've added. Click on the drop-down arrow next to the website that you'd like to place in a folder.

3. I selected Lori's Latest Links. Click on *New Folder* from the pop-up window that appears.

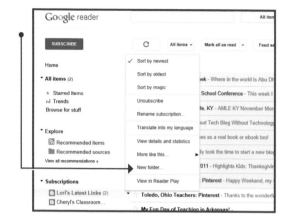

4. The next pop-up window that appears will ask you to name the folder. In the example, I named my folder *Technology*. Click *OK* when you've finished.

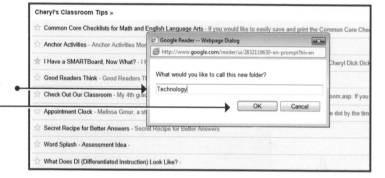

5. Now when you look at the *Subscriptions* section, you'll see the folder you created with the selected website listed under it.

The great thing about Google Reader is you can access it anywhere you have Internet capability. The same page will show whether you are at home, at school, or waiting in the parking lot for your daughter to finish band practice. Talk about professional development on the go!

Look What You Can Do

Watch for the RSS symbol on websites and blogs. RSS stands for Really Simple Syndication. This symbol let's you know that there's an easy way for you to subscribe to that site.

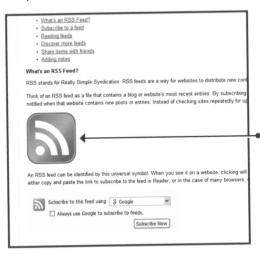

If you see the RSS symbol on a site you want to add to your Google Reader page, click on the icon. You'll either be given the option of adding the site to your Google Reader page, or you'll be given an address to copy and paste once you're logged on to Google Reader.

On some websites and blogs, you'll notice phrases such as *Subscribe* or *Share*. You can also click on those words to link the site to your Google Reader account.

Here are some of the wonderful blogs I subscribe to on my Google Reader: Cheryl's Classroom Tips, Free Technology for Teachers, I Learn Technology, and InTech InSights.

Get Real

Even when you know a website's URL or address, it may not work with Google Reader. If the site isn't set up with a subscription feed, you may not be able to add it to your Reader page. Always look for the RSS symbol or subscription option if you have trouble adding a subscription. If you don't see either, the site may not have the ability to work with Google Reader.

Remember that many schools block blogs due to their security settings. You may not be able to access subscriptions on your Google Reader page at school if your district blocks personal blogs. It would be worth sending a request to your technicians or tech director to have education blogs unblocked.

A QUICK TIP

If you have an iPad, you'll want to use your Google Reader with a fantastic free app called Flipboard. Flipboard is a fast way to literally flip through all the news, people, topics, blogs, and websites you enjoy. Flipboard now has a Google Reader subscription option so you can connect both these tools and read your favorites with a finger swipe. Get the app at http://ax.itunes.apple.com/us/app/flipboard/id358801284?mt=8/.

SOLUTION 3

Find Lessons on Read Write Think

"No! Don't stop. *Please* keep reading." Aren't those words music to your ears? When you get your students excited about reading and they don't want the story to end, you know you're doing something right—and very important. Literacy is the foundation for all of our instruction. Students must be fluent readers and writers to succeed both academically and in our ever-changing world.

If you're like me, then you love literacy instruction. Literature circles, graphic organizers, book talks, writer's workshop, oh, my! I can't help but smile when I think about those things. And I'm constantly on the prowl for new ways to make reading and writing relevant for my students. As our world continues to become more and more digital, it's important to integrate tech tools into the literacy curriculum.

The International Reading Association's position statement (2009) on that subject is clear. "To become fully literate in today's world, students must become proficient in the new literacies of 21st-century technologies. As a result, literacy educators have a responsibility to effectively integrate these new technologies into the curriculum, preparing students for the literacy future they deserve."

Gulp. Are you wondering how you're supposed to do *that*? Relax. Let me introduce you to a website called Read Write Think. Hands down, it is my favorite online literacy resource. There's an entire section on the site dedicated to "Student Interactives," which is chock-full of free technology tools that engage students in online literacy learning. You'll love the ideas in this section.

The site is created by the International Reading Association in partnership with the National Council of Teachers of English, so you know that it's good. Whether you're looking for some really great ideas to use in the classroom or want to brush up on current best literacy practices, this is your go-to site. Are you ready to take a closer look?

Let's Get Started

1. Zip on over to http://www.readwritethink.org/. Notice the different options listed across the top of the home page. You'll see *Classroom Resources*, *Professional Development*, *About Us*, and *Parent & Afterschool Resources*.

2. For this tour of the site, let's check out all of the options listed under the *Classroom Resources* section.

3. Roll your mouse over the *Classroom Resources* option to activate a drop-down menu. Click on the *Lesson Plans* option.

FIND A LESSON

1. Locate the search bar on the left-hand side of the screen. Here you can search for any type of literacy lesson you need. Just type in your topic and then click on the orange *Go* button.

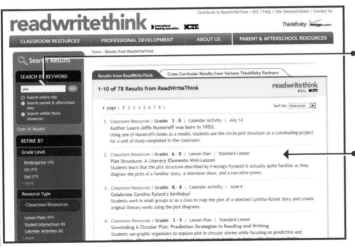

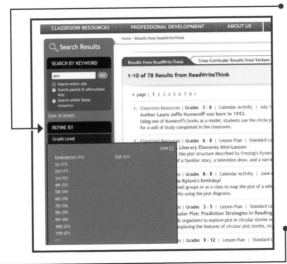

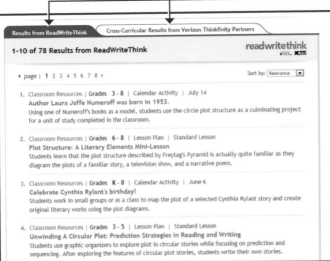

2. For example, let's say I want to find a lesson for teaching Plot. I type "plot" in the search bar and click the *Go* button. All of the lessons that focus on plot will appear in the middle of the page.

3. To narrow down the choices by grade level, look to the left-hand side of the screen. Under the heading *Refine By,* find the option *Grade Level.* Click on the appropriate grade level.

4. Notice the two tabs on the upper part of the screen. One tab is labeled *Results from Read Write Think*; the other tab is labeled *Cross-Curricular Results from Verizon Thinkfinity Partners.*

5. To search strictly for literacy lessons, stay on the *Read Write Think* tab. For ideas on how to tie your topic into another subject area, click on the *Cross-Curricular* tab. It's a great feature, but for this tour, let's stay on the *Read Write Think* tab.

6. Awesome. Now you have a list of lessons that pertain to your grade level and topic. Select one to consider by clicking on the title of the lesson.

TAKE A CLOSER LOOK

1. In my example, I've selected a lesson about teaching circular plot. Here you'll see an overview of the lesson.

2. For each lesson, there are tabs you can click on for additional information. The tabs are labeled *Preview, Standards, Resources & Preparation, Instructional Plan, Related Resources,* and *Comments.*

3. Let's say I wanted to know more about the *Resources & Preparation* necessary for the lesson I selected; I'd just click on that tab.

4. Look, this is great. A student interactive tool is used in this lesson. Students will not only get instruction from me, but they can practice their skills using a web tool they'll enjoy. Interactives are the main reason this is my favorite literacy instruction site.

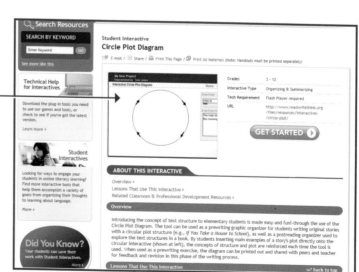

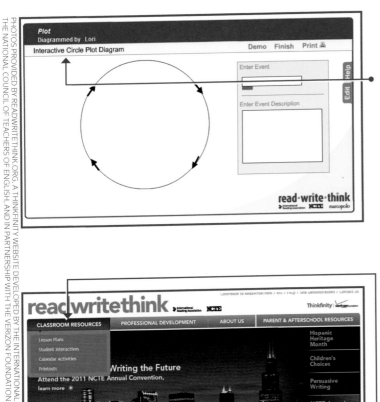

5. Using interactives, I'm able to teach my literacy curriculum and present it in a way that students love. I don't have to chase all over the web either; everything is nice and organized for me in one place. You've gotta love that.

SEARCH FOR STUDENT INTERACTIVES

1. So, we know you can quickly and easily search for lessons by typing your topic in the search bar. What else is on this site?

2. Go to the top of the page and roll your mouse over the *Classroom Resources* option again. Now click on the *Student Interactives* option. Here you'll find engaging simulations or games to use with your own literacy lessons.

3. A list of all the student interactives will appear in the middle of your screen.

4. You can scroll through the list or use the *Search Resources* menu on the left-hand side of the screen again to refine your search.

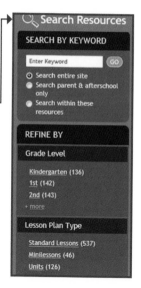

5. Read Write Think provides interactives for all grade levels. Everyone can find something good to use with her class. Here are a few of my favorites.

6. For grades K–2, there is the Picture Match game. Students match pictures and beginning sounds.

7. All grade levels will have fun putting their writing skills to good use with the Comic Creator.

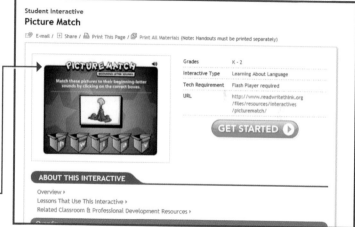

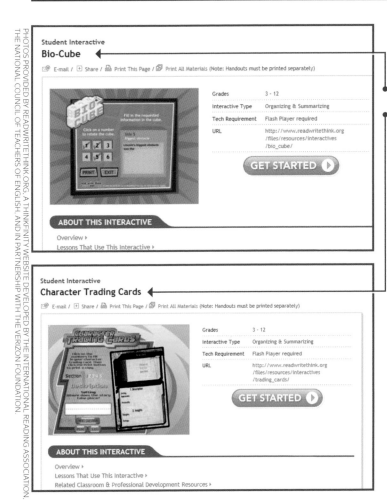

8. You can check for reading comprehension of a story by having students create a Bio-Cube or Character Trading Cards.

9. Do you think your students will be excited to use these resources on the interactive whiteboard or computer instead of filling in a worksheet? I'm pretty sure the response would be yes.

GET INSPIRED WITH CALENDAR ACTIVITIES

1. Let's keep checking out what's available on Read Write Think. Roll your mouse over the *Classroom Resources* option once again. This time click on *Calendar Activities* from the menu.

2. For each day of the year, Read Write Think provides you with a special reason to celebrate the day. It might be a nationally recognized day such as National Ice Cream Day, a famous person's birthday, or facts about a holiday.

3. I really like this feature. I often incorporate the information I find here in my Morning Message, or I use the information to come up with ideas for student journal writing assignments.

4. To learn more about the day's celebration, click on its title. For each event, Read Write Think offers four levels of information: *Event Description, Classroom Activity, Websites,* and *Related Resources.*

TIME-SAVING PRINTOUTS

1. Is there still more? You bet. Go back to *Classroom Resources,* and this time click on *Printouts.*

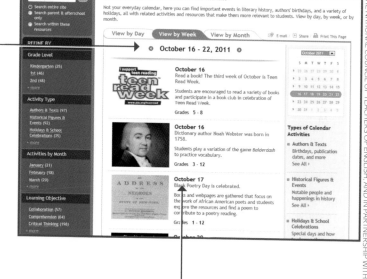

PHOTOS PROVIDED BY READWRITETHINK.ORG, A THINKFINITY WEBSITE DEVELOPED BY THE INTERNATIONAL READING ASSOCIATION, THE NATIONAL COUNCIL OF TEACHERS OF ENGLISH, AND IN PARTNERSHIP WITH THE VERIZON FOUNDATION.

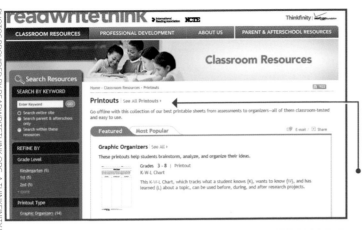

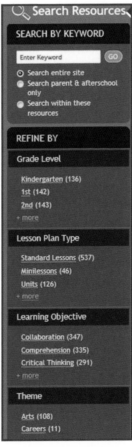

2. Even though we're all trying to go paperless, there will always be times when you need a graphic organizer or review sheet. Read Write Think provides hundreds of printable resources to use with your instruction.

3. Again you can sort through the printouts by using the *Search Resources* menu on the left-hand side of the screen to refine your search.

4. You'll find a K-W-L chart, an editor's checklist, poetry frames, and many others. Click on the title of the sheet to learn more about it.

5. For every printout, Read Write Think offers three levels of information: *Teaching with this Printout*, *More Ideas to Try*, and *Related Resources*.

6. Can you understand why I really enjoy using this site? It has so many wonderful resources in one place.

Look What You Can Do

Use the *Parent & Afterschool Resources* area listed at the top of the home page to educate parents in ways they can help their children with reading and writing. You can e-mail the links to parents or paste them to your website. Parents will appreciate these simple guides and ideas for helping their children at home.

Read Write Think added a *Save* feature to several of the Student Interactives. Students may not be able to complete an activity in one sitting, so the ability to save their work is helpful. You'll know an interactive can be saved by looking for the *Save* tab on the start-up page for the interactive. For example, the Acrostic Poem interactive can be saved. When a student needs to save his work he clicks on the *Save* tab.

When the work is saved, it will be saved in the Read Write Think (RWT) format. Students will need to name their work and click on the orange *Save* button.

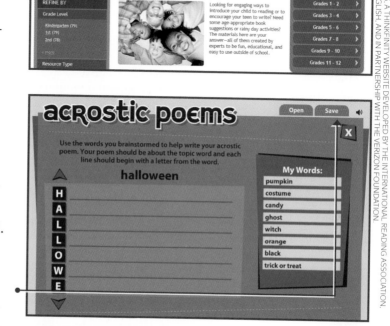

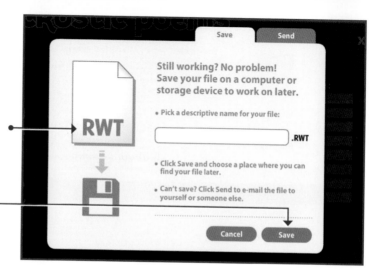

PHOTOS PROVIDED BY READWRITETHINK.ORG, A THINKFINITY WEBSITE DEVELOPED BY THE INTERNATIONAL READING ASSOCIATION, THE NATIONAL COUNCIL OF TEACHERS OF ENGLISH, AND IN PARTNERSHIP WITH THE VERIZON FOUNDATION.

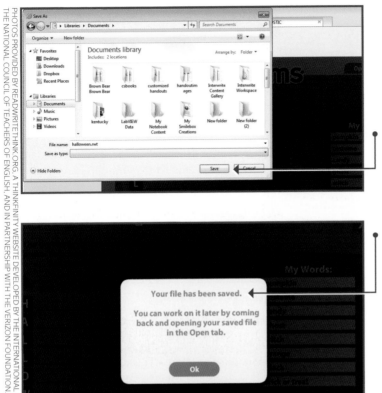

The site will ask where you'd like to save the file. Maybe you want students to save it to the computer, a flash drive, or a shared file for your class. Select the location and click that *Save* button.

You'll see a confirmation message on the screen verifying that the work has been saved. In order to edit or revise work, online access is necessary. The file opens in the Read Write Think website.

You can also print out the completed work or send it to an e-mail address. After you click on the *Save* tab of an interactive, a pop-up screen will appear. Click on *Send* to e-mail the work to a student's parent or send it to yourself so that you can assess it at a later time.

Get Real

One technical detail you want to check on before using the interactives with students is to make sure your Flash player is updated on the computers. Read Write Think uses Flash from Adobe for their interactives. Just make sure Flash is up-to-date so students won't get frustrated. There's one other bump in the road. If you're using an iPad or iPod touch in your classroom, Flash does not work on those devices.

A QUICK TIP

Read Write Think has a direct link to all of the plug-in tools your students will need to fully utilize the site. Plug-in tools are applications like Flash, Shockwave, and QuickTime. These tools make the games interactive and provide special effects. To update your plug-ins, visit http://www.readwritethink.org/util/help.html/.

Create Rubrics Using RubiStar

You're probably familiar with the term rubric. Professor Heidi Andrade offered this clear definition in her 2008 article, *Self-Assessment Through Rubrics,* "A rubric is a scoring tool that lists the criteria for a piece of work, or 'what counts' (for example, purpose, organization, details, voice, and mechanics are often what count in a piece of writing); it also articulates gradations of quality for each criterion, from excellent to poor." To oversimply things a bit, I like to think of it this way: a rubric sets up the target I need to shoot for.

When we assign projects or more involved assignments, both students and parents appreciate having a rubric. That way, everyone is on the same page about the specific guidelines and our expectations for the finished piece of work. With a rubric, there's no guesswork, and there are no surprises.

Even though we know rubrics are important and helpful, sometimes we shy away from making them because they can be tedious and frustrating to create. RubiStar is one of the very first web tools I ever used. I learned about it years ago while receiving some professional development training for myself. Someone shared how they could create top-notch rubrics for their students in just minutes. I was intrigued. I had experienced the agony of not only deciding what should go into a rubric, but the difficulty of formatting the page so that everything would look presentable.

RubiStar was, and still is, such a help to me as I create rubrics to facilitate and assess learning. I think you'll find this site extremely easy to use. It may even encourage you to use more rubrics in your classroom. Ready to learn more?

Let's Get Started

RubiStar is supported by a grant from the U.S. Department of Education. It doesn't cost you anything to use it. To get started you just need to register for an account.

GET AN ACCOUNT

1. Go to http://rubistar.4teachers.org/. Look at the top right-hand corner of the screen. Click on either *Register* or *Sign Up*. They both take you to the same place.

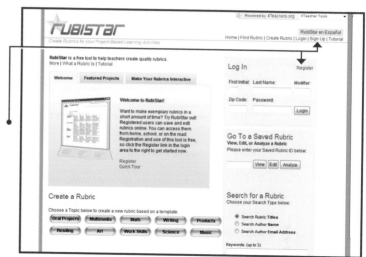

2. Fill in your title, first initial, last name, zip code, password, and e-mail address. Then click on the green *Register* button.

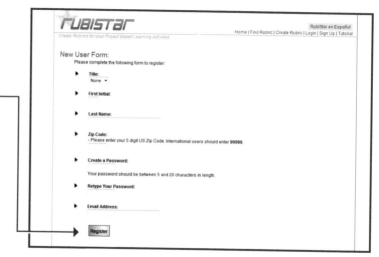

3. The next screen will confirm that your account has been set up. You can now start your first rubric. Click on the square in the middle of the page that says *New Rubric*.

CHOOSE A TYPE OF RUBRIC

1. You will see lists of all existing rubrics available. They're organized by different types of projects and subject areas.

2. If you select from one of the lists, you'll begin with an already created template. If you'd rather create one from scratch, scroll to the very bottom of that page and click on the *Click Here to Create a Brand New Rubric* option.

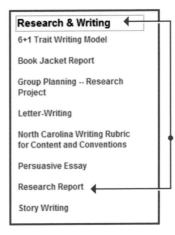

3. From my experience, it's much easier to start with a general template than to start from scratch. So for my example I'm going to select a *Research Report* rubric from the *Research & Writing* category.

4. Once you click on the type of rubric you want to create, you'll see a page where you name and design your rubric. My name is already showing here because I'm logged in to the account.

5. You need to name the rubric and type in your zip code. Entering your zip code helps RubiStar collect data for the grant that's providing the funding for this site.

6. Some teachers create a rubric, print it out, and are finished.

7. Others want to save it in their RubiStar accounts to use again later. Click on the drop-down arrow under *Demonstration Rubric* and choose either *Yes, my rubric is a temporary rubric*, or *No, my rubric is a permanent rubric*.

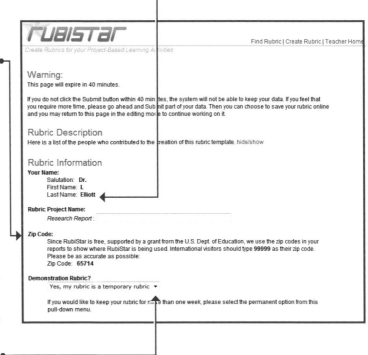

CONSTRUCT YOUR RUBRIC

1. Scroll down the page. Here's where you actually construct your rubric. Look at the column on the left-hand side of the chart. Notice the *Please Choose* heading in every row.

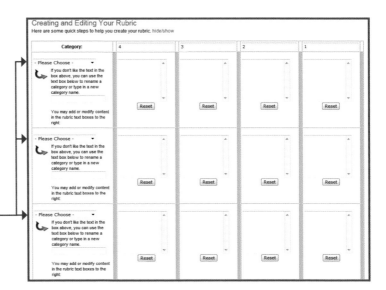

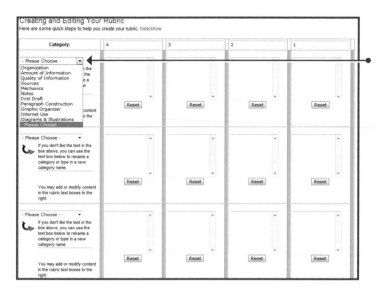

2. Click on the drop-down arrow next to the first *Please Choose* heading to view the criteria categories already created for this type of rubric. Select the one you want by clicking on it.

3. After you click on an option, each box in the row will fill with a description of how the criteria will be scored.

4. If you like the wording of the scoring descriptions, then just leave them alone. If you want to change something, simply highlight the words you want to change, delete them, and type in your own words.

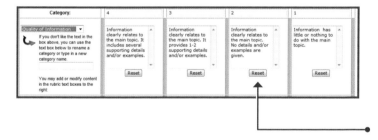

5. In my example, I chose the *Quality of Information* as the criteria category. You can see the descriptions for how that criteria will be scored, as a 4, 3, 2, or 1 across the row.

CUSTOMIZE THE CRITERIA

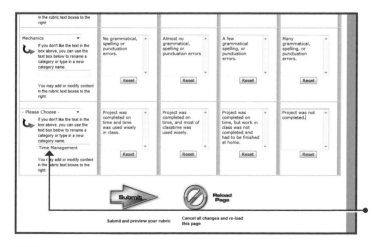

1. If you want to customize the criteria instead of selecting a choice from the drop-down menu, simply type your heading into the text box under *Please Choose*.

2. You'll also need to type in your own scoring descriptions across the row for each of the rating areas. In my sample, I added Time Management as the criteria and then typed in descriptors for each scoring level.

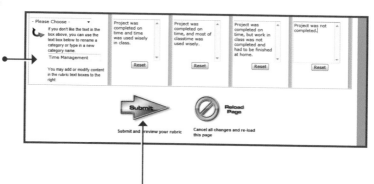

3. When you're finished selecting all of the criteria for your rubric, go to the bottom of the screen and click on the arrow-shaped *Submit* button.

PREVIEW, PRINT & SAVE YOUR RUBRIC

1. The next window will show you your rubric. Look how nice and organized it looks. You can edit it by clicking on the green *Modify This Rubric* button at the top of the page.

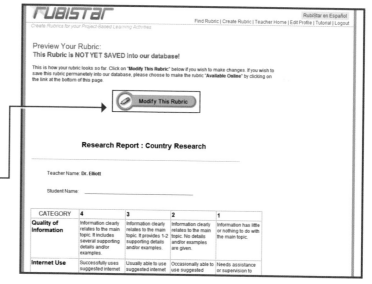

2. Now that you've previewed your rubric and possibly made changes to it, you can print it or download it.

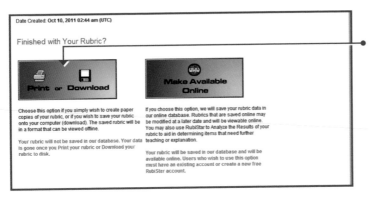

3. Scroll to the bottom of the preview and click on the green *Print or Download* button. Notice the consequences associated with the finishing options.

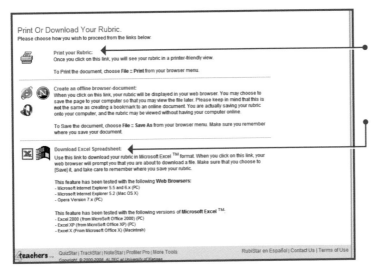

4. Here, you'll either want to click on the first option to print your rubric or the third one to save it on your computer as an Excel spreadsheet. The middle option of saving it as an offline browser document probably isn't one you'll use.

SAVE YOUR RUBRIC ONLINE

1. You can also make the rubric available online for your students and other teachers to use. To do this, click on the blue *Make Available Online* button.

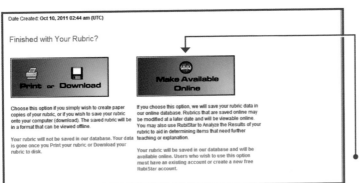

2. When you choose this option, RubiStar will save the rubric to your account and assign it an identification number. This is how you, and others, can gain access to it.

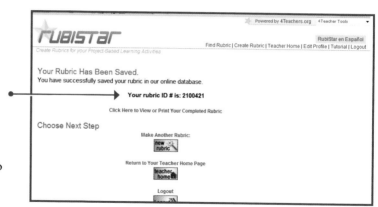

3. To find your rubric, go to RubiStar's home page. Look to the right-hand side of the screen and enter the ID# in the box under the heading *Go To a Saved Rubric*. Then click on the *View* button.

4. Alternately, at the top of the RubiStar home page, you can click on the *Teacher Home* option. This will take you to your account and show you all of the rubrics that you've saved. You can then edit the rubrics or print them from here.

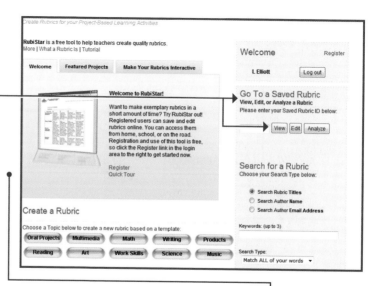

5. Fantastic! You can create a valuable assessment tool in just a few minutes.

6. Having the ability to save the rubrics in your account also allows you to reuse or edit them as necessary. Providing students guidelines and targets for learning has never been easier.

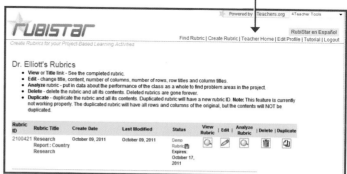

Look What You Can Do

Now that you have the basics down, why not try customizing your rubrics even more. Go to the RubiStar home page. Look at the top of the page and click on *Teacher Home*. You'll see your account and a list of the rubrics you've saved. To edit a rubric, click on the icon of a pencil under the word *Edit*.

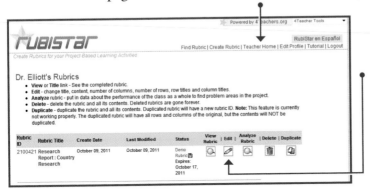

You can now edit the columns, row names, or contents of your rubric. Just click on the appropriate button and RubiStar will walk you through the steps.

If, for example, you don't want to use a 4, 3, 2, 1 scale but would prefer to label the columns *Advanced*, *Proficient*, and *Basic*, you'd click on the *Edit Columns* button and make those changes.

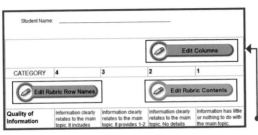

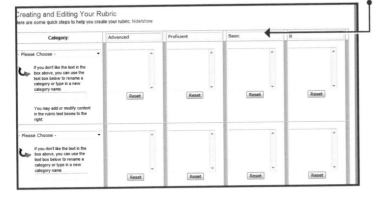

You may want to try your hand at constructing a rubric from scratch after you've used several. Click on *Create Rubric,* which can be found at the top of any RubiStar page. Scroll to the bottom of the page and click on *Create a Rubric from Scratch.* Once you select that option, RubiStar will lead you step-by-step through the process.

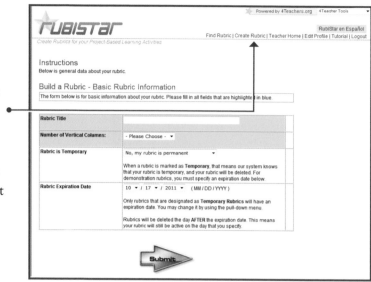

Use rubrics in your writing instruction. Prepare rubrics for several different types of writing genres ahead of time. Make the different rubrics available in folders in your writing center. As students work on various writing projects, they'll be able to access the expectations for that particular type of writing genre.

Before assigning students a research project, construct rubrics for all of the different research project options you'll make available. Let students see the rubrics for each type of project before they commit to a project. Knowing what type of work will be required for a certain project ahead of time can provide for differentiation and ownership of the learning.

You may have English language learners in your classroom. RubiStar provides an option for creating and publishing your rubrics in Spanish. This is a nice feature because it allows you to share your rubrics with Spanish-speaking parents. At the very top of the RubiStar page you'll see *RubiStar in Espanol.* When you click on this, the text will convert to Spanish. Just click on *RubiStar in English* to return to English text.

A QUICK TIP

RubiStar has a partner website that provides an online quiz maker. QuizStar not only creates quizzes, but after a student takes a quiz online, QuizStar automatically grades the quiz. Assessment doesn't seem quite so taxing now, does it? Visit http://quizstar.4teachers.org/.

Get Real

Don't be surprised when you use a rubric for the first time if it doesn't address everything you need. Sometimes you have to tweak rubrics once you have students actually using them. This is why it's important to save your RubiStar rubrics in your account.

And please don't find yourself saying, "Help! I know I saved that rubric, but it's disappeared from my account." Remember when you first begin constructing a rubric you need to click on the *No, my rubric is a permanent rubric* option if you want the rubric to stay in your account. If you choose *Yes, my rubric is a temporary rubric*, RubiStar will only store it for one week due to the high number of teachers who use the service.

Engaging the Digital Generation

Have you joined the thousands of people who are addicted to playing the game Angry Birds? I'd never been a video game person in my life until Angry Birds. I have the basic version, Seasons, and even the Rio edition. The birds are all over my iPhone and iPad. What's the deal with flinging our feathered friends via a slingshot on a mission to destroy pigs, monkeys, or other things? I'm really not a violent person, but I can spend oodles of time getting caught up in the craziness. Why? First, I want to get to the next level. Accomplishing a task successfully and then being challenged with another one is motivating. Second, I want to get the high score. It's not good enough just to move on. I want to see all the stars blinking at me and see that high-score message flashing. But most of all, I've discovered that I really love to strategize my next move. Because I've played so many different versions and levels, I'm getting pretty good at predicting what strategies will work. Trial-and-error teaches me something each time. The birds have me hooked.

Is This Entertainment or Engagement?

Games tend to engage us and draw us in. While playing, we actually learn new information or skills. Students seem to perk up when we introduce a game into a lesson. It's like a switch is flipped on, and engagement levels rise. I can understand this because of my own experience with Angry Birds. Games are novel. They break the monotony of our routine. The best ones challenge us to strategize, reward us with new levels when we achieve, and pat us on the back by celebrating our win or high scores. Video games have been a part of our culture since the 1980s. Remember PacMan and Donkey Kong? Of course today's video games are much more colorful, interactive, and challenging. Many of them require problem-solving and even collaboration with others. Because video games and interactive experiences are not only motivating to students, but a part of their lives outside of school, why not bring those formats into the classroom?

James Gee, a professor at the University of Wisconsin-Madison, has been researching video games and learning for many years now. He recognizes the higher level of engagement video games provide. In his 2005 article, "Good Video Games and Good Learning," he stated, "Challenge and learning are a large part of what makes good video games motivating and entertaining. Humans actually enjoy learning, though sometimes in school you wouldn't know that." I know lots of students who spend hours outside of school perfecting their Halo skills, dancing moves with Wii, or planning football plays with Madden.

This may sound very exciting, but the reality of implementing video games in the classroom on a regular basis seems very untraditional. But how and why would you want to integrate the whole nature of gaming and the use of other interactive technologies into your classroom?

Teaching 21st-Century Skills

The Partnership for 21st-Century Skills and other education organizations are stressing the need for education to go beyond the simple recall of facts to develop skills such as critical thinking and creativity. Sir Ken Robinson, in his book *The Element: How Finding Your Passion Changes Everything*, strongly encourages educators to fuel creativity. "Creativity [is] as important as literacy, and we should treat it with the same status." Wow, as important as literacy? For students to succeed, they'll need to learn how to think and think creatively. In college we all studied Bloom's

Taxonomy. In the updated version from the 1990s, the highest levels of thinking involve evaluating and creating. Notice how those new terms are verbs. Students need to be actively engaged in their learning.

Where Do I Begin?

Using technology can help us weave 21st-century skills into our daily instruction. Technology provides us with some amazing tools that students can use to produce incredible products. Instead of filling in a worksheet, answering yet another set of questions, or listening to a lecture, students can explore, research, and apply those same concepts to a new product.

Of course teaching students to think creatively and critically doesn't mean that they must use technology. When you help students set their own learning goals or use real-world scenarios for them to solve in their math lessons, you're teaching them to use these skills. But learning is fun, and purposely weaving game playing or an interactive technology into our day can be very rewarding. We've come a long way from Heads Up, Seven Up, and Spelling Bees, yet students still enjoy those games. So why not introduce a whole new set of games and other online resources into your repertoire? We're so lucky to be teachers today. There are so many free, high-quality resources available to us at our fingertips—quite literally.

In this chapter I'll introduce you to Arcademic Skill Builders and VocabularySpellingCity. You, your students, and their parents will love these sites because they are very motivational, and they'll support and supplement your curriculum beautifully. As we prepare our students to become successful learners in the 21st century, we need to embrace the tools that our students—the generation of digital learners—will be using throughout their lives.

Compete on Arcademic Skill Builders

As a kid, the first gaming system in my house was Atari. My brother got one for Christmas and played Space Invaders incessantly. There was just something about shooting at aliens that captured an entire generation. When you look at images of those old games, you realize how far we've come with technology. Makes you wonder where we'll be in another 20 years. The games today are so colorful and have real scenarios. As a player, the incentives to beat your high scores are better than ever. And instead of just mindless shooting, there are so many engaging and educational games out there. Imagine having a Wii or Play Station system loaded with classroom games for your students. That would be pretty cool, huh?

Well, here's an alternative. You can use free, high-quality games online. Let me introduce you to Arcademic Skill Builders. Originally created in the research department of the University of Kansas School of Education, Arcademic Skill Builders is built on the idea that fun, timed practice of basic math facts leads to increased fluency for students. The site's creators also believe that multiplayer competition engages students and pushes them to achieve. Turns out they were right. In 2009, Arcademics won a National Science Foundation (NSF) grant to develop and test multiplayer math games in the classroom, and the results were impressive.

Now supported by the NSF and the International Society for Technology in Education, Arcademic Skill Builders offers students multiperson games to practice math skills. This means that while your students are playing a game, they can actually compete with other students from your class, or from around the world. Talk about motivating! And you can rest assured that the site is completely secure. No one has or can access your students online. I like that kind of safety. Ready, set, go—let's play!

Let's Get Started

Arcademic Skill Builders a free site. You don't even need to register to play the games. I really like that feature. Students simply go to the site and select the game they want to play. I'll walk you through the set-up process, and then you can teach your students how to do it.

SELECT A GAME

1. Go to http://www.arcademicskillbuilders.com/. Look across the middle of the screen. In the yellow band you'll see the math games listed by specific skills. There are a few geography, language arts, and typing games available, too.

2. To demonstrate how the site works, I'll walk you through how to play the Penguin Jump Multiplication game.

3. Look in the yellow band across the middle of the screen and click on the word *Multiplication*. You'll see all of the multiplication games displayed. Find the one with the picture of the penguins and click on the blue arrow that says *Play*.

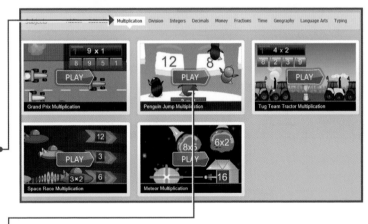

4. This will take you to the actual game. Click on the blue *Play* arrow to set up the game.

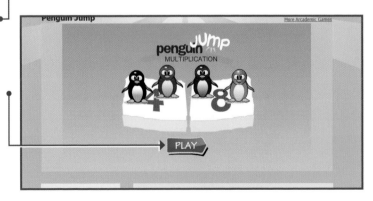

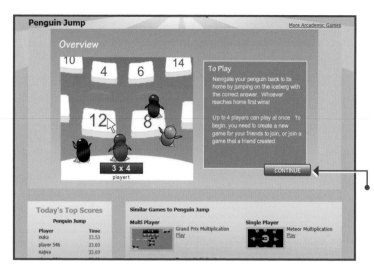

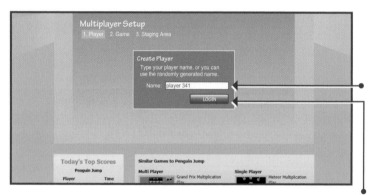

CHOOSE A PLAYER NAME

1. On the left-hand side of the screen you'll see a screenshot from the game. On the right-hand side you'll see an overview of the game. Click on the blue *Continue* button after you read the description.

2. Students need a player name in order to see their scores at the end of the game. Students can use the randomly generated name provided here or type in their own nickname.

3. Students love typing in nicknames, but in this example I'll keep the player name provided, player 341. Click on the blue *Login* button when the name is ready.

PUBLIC OR PRIVATE?

1. Arcademic is so popular because students can compete against others. Students can join a game already in progress or create one of their own.

2. Look at the chart in the middle of the screen. In this example, you'll notice that another student is already playing the Penguin Jump game. Find the small tabs on the top right-hand side of the window that say *Public* and *Private*.

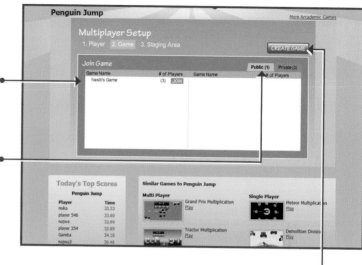

3. If a game is public, then anyone online who wants to play can join the fun. A private game requires a password to participate.

4. Click on the blue *Create Game* button at the top right-hand side of the screen.

5. Now's the time to make the decision about making the game public or private. If you click on the circle next to the words *Public Game,* then anyone can join your game.

6. If you click on the circle next to the words *Private Game*, a Password box will appear. You'll need to create a password for your private game and then click on the *Next* button. You'll share this password with your students.

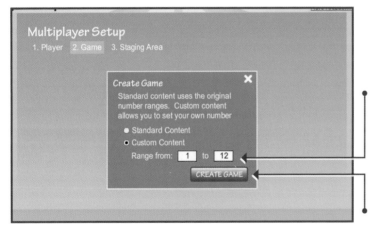

GET SET

1. Your final option is to decide whether you want to use *Standard* or *Custom* content.

2. If you choose the *Standard Content* option, the game will include problems using the standard number range for this skill. To see what the standard range is, click on the *Custom Content* option.

3. The *Custom Content* option allows you to type in the number range you'd like to target. This is a really nice option because it lets you customize the game to focus on skills you want your students to practice. Decide on content and click on *Create Game*.

GO!

1. Let's play already. It may seem like a lot of steps just to get those penguins jumping, but the more you use the site, the faster this process will go. Students just click right through and are ready to play in seconds.

2. You're ready to rumble! Click on *Start Race* to begin. There will be a five-second countdown, and then the game will begin. Go penguins go!

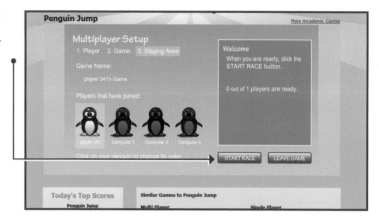

3. Problems will appear in the blue box at the bottom of the screen. Students click on the ice chunk that displays the correct answer. If they make a mistake, the penguin falls in the water. Then he's right back up and ready to try that same problem again.

4. Students keep going until their penguins reach the finish line.

AND THE WINNER IS

1. The purpose of the game is to become fluent and fast with the multiplication facts. A student's score is based on time and accuracy. The final screen shows a student her score and where she placed compared to the others playing the same game.

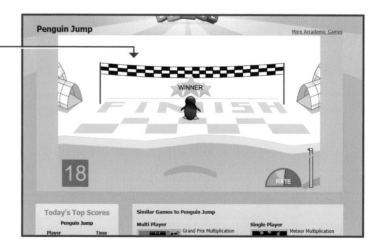

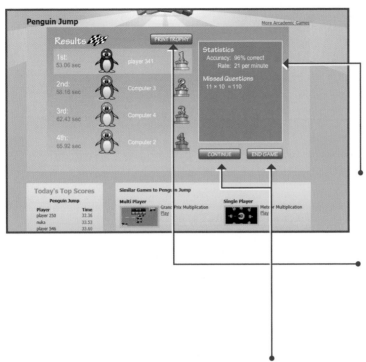

2. The box on the bottom left-hand corner of the screen shows Today's Top Scores. Find the Statistics box at the top right-hand side of the window. Here a student can see how many problems he answered correctly and which ones he missed.

3. At the top of the window, there is a *Print Trophy* button. If you want students to print and keep track of their accomplishments, they can print the certificates provided.

4. Do you want to quit or keep playing? Click on *Continue* to play another round of this game or *End Game* to choose something else or stop playing.

5. What do you think? Will your students want to compete in this way while learning key skills? It really is a lot of fun. I found myself playing the Penguin Jump game again and again trying to beat my own time.

Look What You Can Do

So what does this really look like when you take your first-grade class to the computer lab to review math facts? First, make sure to pre-assess and determine the skill levels of your students. Then, place students in groups of four. They will play against each other using the games you've selected. I suggest that, prior to heading down to the lab, you take a few minutes to select a leader for each group, your Tech Assistants. You will need the Tech Assistants to actually set up a game for their group because Arcademic Skill Builders has a time limit for the private games, so creating them ahead of time usually doesn't work. Feeling a little uneasy about using students as assistants? They really are very capable, even at a young age, of working through the set-up process. Make sure to choose your leaders and take time to model the process prior to going to the lab and involve all the students. Also, prepare a scoring sheet for each student to record her scores.

Instruct your Tech Assistants so they know which private game they need to organize for their group. If they need to customize the range, make sure to help them when they get to that step in the process. Use the same process described earlier in the chapter for creating a private game. A first-grade group might play Kitten Match, Jet Ski, or Tub Team Tugboat to practice addition facts. Members of each group of four sit near each other in the lab. While students wait for the assistant to set up the private game, have them practice using the one-person game. The single-person game for addition practice is Alien Addition. The Tech Assistants quickly set up the games and then tell their teammates when to start. At the end of the game, the students record their scores. They can continue to replay the same game, or you may have them try out another game with your Tech Assistant again getting things ready.

If you really don't want to have students assist in the process of set-ting up the private games, you can have all the students work on the single-player games while you quickly set up the various private games. As long as everyone is engaged while things are being prepared, it should work either way.

Not all students in third grade have mastered their multiplication facts, so set up various games with different number fact ranges and have students within the class compete with each other. Differentiated instruc-tion has never been easier. Everybody is having a good time, and each student is working on his level. If you have an interactive whiteboard, Arcademic Skill Builders is a perfect site to have students use while they work in small groups at the board.

Another way you can use Arcademic Skill Build-ers is to encourage it as a resource for home. Parents are always looking for safe places their children can go on the computer. Share this resource on your website  and newsletters. Assign player names so you can watch the leader board on the home page of the website to see if any of your students are listed. Once the class sees one of their own on that home page, the motivation to

A QUICK TIP

Have a plan when using Arcademic Skill Builders with your students. Link the site to your website for easy access. Assign each student specific skill areas they should stay in to avoid aimless game playing. Require students to record their scores and the statistics for each game. If you're concerned about accountability, then place students in pairs and have them record each other's scores.

do better is immediately instilled. Everyone wants to be a star, and there is just something about seeing your name, even if it's a nickname, on a website.

Get Real

As you peruse the Arcademic site, those of you who teach fifth and sixth grades may be a little concerned about your students getting charged up about penguins and kittens. I hear you. There are some very cutesy images on some of the games, but keep looking. There are also race cars, meteors, and space-related games. With any website, try it out with students and if they moan and groan, then try something else. If they giggle and stay focused, keep using it.

You may face a problem getting the games to play because of your district's firewall. The firewall is one way to protect your computers from digital viruses that can be spread by visiting certain Internet sites. Arcademic has thought of this also. If you run into difficulties, share the following link with your IT folks: http://www.arcademicskillbuilders.com/firewall/.

Motivate Using VocabularySpellingCity

One day my second-grade teacher challenged me to learn to spell a list of very big words and "encyclopedia" was the first one on the list. I loved the challenge. I read, spelled, chanted, wrote, and even sang the word. En-cy-clo-ped-ia. To me learning to spell new words was just as much fun as recess was to other kids.

To this day, I still love reading, writing, and spelling. But many of my students don't love words the way I do. They feel that spelling is more of a chore than a hobby. Over the years I've tried to make learning new spelling words exciting by having Spelling Bees, playing Sparkle, and filling in sticker charts for perfect scores on tests. But nothing has quite hit the mark the way VocabularySpellingCity does.

Students love it because they get to play games and challenge them-selves. Teachers love it because students are having fun learning. Parents love it because it takes the frustration out of quizzing their kids before a test. VocabularySpellingCity is a snap to use. You just type in your spell-ing list, and the site generates games and activities for students to play using your words. Students can access the lists and activities from their computers at home. When students take a test online, the program will say each word aloud and use it in a sentence. You can even customize the sentences to make them meaningful to your class. Talk about engage-ment! VocabularySpellingCity sits at the top of my list of best-learning sites. Ready to get started? Let's go!

Let's Get Started

VocabularySpellingCity is a free online spelling service. If you want access to additional features, including vocabulary practice, you'll need to upgrade to a paid membership. I'll walk you through how to use the free version, and then you'll be able to show your students how to use the site.

REGISTER FOR AN ACCOUNT

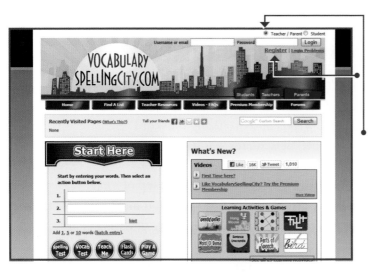

1. Go to http://www. spellingcity.com/. The first step is to register. Look at the top right-hand side of the screen. Select the circle next to Teacher/Parent and then click on *Register*.

2. You'll need to fill in your full name, a username, an e-mail address, and a password. Keep the box under Password checked only if you want to receive news from the site. On the right-hand side of the screen, click on the *I Am a Teacher* option.

3. After you click on the circle next to teacher, a message will pop up to help you locate your school. Click on the blue words *Find My School*.

4. When the next window appears, type in your school's zip code, and then click on *Find My School*.

5. A list will appear. Locate your school on the list. Click on the name of the school.

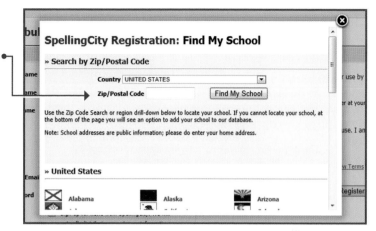

6. After clicking on your school's name, you'll be taken back to the registration page. Click on the blue text that says *View Terms*. If you agree to the site's terms, then click on the *Register* button.

7. The next screen looks very busy, but don't get overwhelmed. The site is trying to get you to consider upgrading to their paid version. At the top of the screen, click on the words in blue that say *No Thanks. I'm OK with the free version for now.*

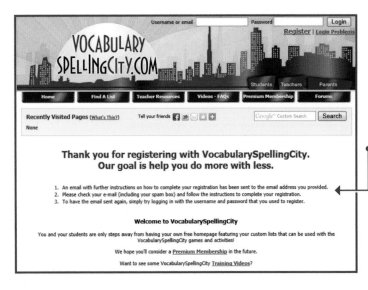

ACTIVATE YOUR ACCOUNT

1. You'll now see a screen that thanks you for registering. You'll also be directed to check your e-mail account to confirm your registration.

2. Take a moment to check your e-mail. VocabularySpellingCity will have sent you a message containing a link. Click on the link. That will activate your account and take you back to their site.

3. You'll see a new screen announcing that your account and home page have been activated. To begin making your lists, fill in your username or e-mail and your password and then click on the *Login* button.

THE TEACHER'S TOOLBOX

1. When you're logged in, look at the top right-hand corner of the page and find the *Teacher Toolbox*.

2. This is where you'll go to put your spelling lists online for your students. Click on *List Management*.

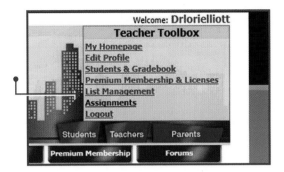

3. Under the bold words *List Management* click on the words written in blue that say *Create a New List*.

CREATE A SPELLING LIST

1. This looks easy enough. At the top of the page you'll type in the name of your list. I called mine *Fall Words*. To choose your grade level, click on the arrow next to *Grade Level* and make your selection from the drop-down menu. I chose 3rd grade.

2. Under *Grade Level* is a box where you can type in a short description of your list. I typed in Week 9.

3. Next you'll type your spelling words in the boxes next to the numbers. I typed in five fall-themed words.

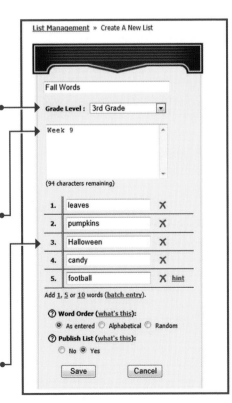

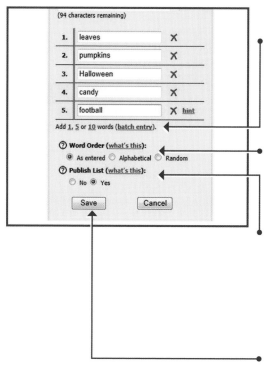

4. To add more spelling words, look below the list and click on *Add 1, 5, or 10 Words*.

5. Notice the *Word Order* option. You can select to have the words appear as you typed them, in alphabetical order, or randomly. Click on the circle next to your choice.

6. You also have the option to *Publish* the list. Publishing a list makes it available to students online. It's probably the choice you want unless you're working weeks ahead. Click on the *Save* button when you're finished.

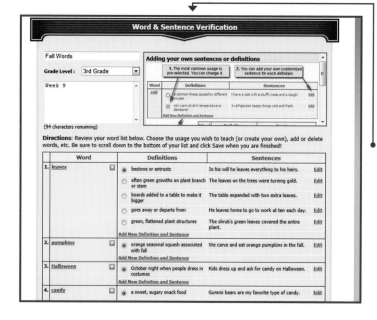

CUSTOMIZE YOUR LIST

1. When students take their spelling tests online, the program will say the word aloud and read a sentence to help the students. On the *Word & Sentence Verification* page, you can select or customize the sentences you want read to your students.

2. I love this feature because you can write sentences that are meaningful to your students. You can rewrite the sentences to include student names, school events, or class information.

3. Look through the list of definitions and sentences offered for each spelling word. If there's more than one option listed, click on the circle next to the choice you want to use.

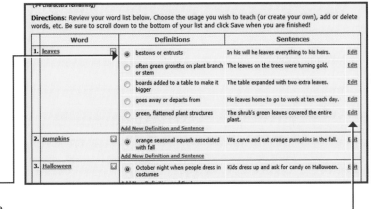

4. To customize a sentence click on the word *Edit* at the end of the sentence you want to change.

5. A pop-up window will open. Type your sentence in the box provided and then click on the *Save* button.

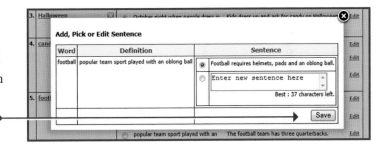

6. Notice in my example I changed the sentence about football so it would relate to my school.

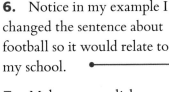

7. Make sure to click on the *Save* button when you have finished editing all of your sentences.

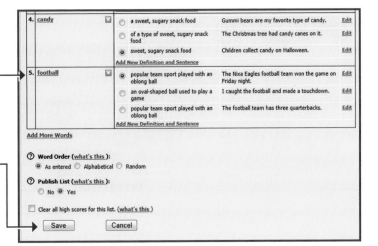

MANAGE YOUR LISTS

1. After saving the list, you'll be shown your account. Notice the section for *Lists*. Each time you add a new spelling list it will be stored here.

2. This is also the place where you can change the status of a published list from *Yes* to *No* or vice versa. Your other options here are to *Edit* your list, *Play* a game, *Print* the list, or *Delete* it.

3. Pretty awesome, right? So, how do students find your lists to practice, play, or test?

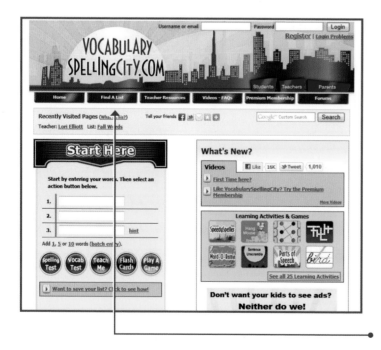

HOW STUDENTS ACCESS THE LISTS

1. When a student goes to http://www.spelling city.com/, she doesn't need to log in (unless you've upgraded to the paid version). The student just looks at the navy buttons across the top of the screen and clicks on the one that says *Find a List*.

2. Next the student needs to type in your name, as you registered it, in the Search box and then click on the *Search* button.

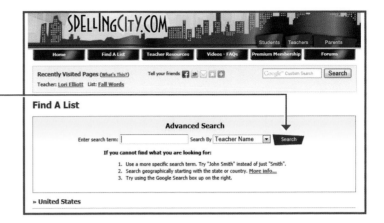

3. VocabularySpelling-City will then show your name and school in a chart at the bottom of the page. The student should click on your name.

4. Your spelling lists will show in the next window. Notice the *Fall Words* list I created in my account.

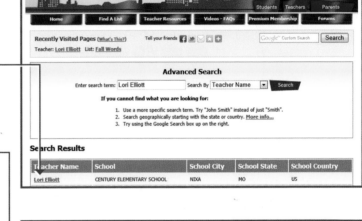

TAKE A TEST

1. A student can take a spelling test by clicking on *S-Test*, review words by clicking on *Teach*, or play games by clicking on *Games*. The vocabulary test (*V-Test*) is not available in the free version.

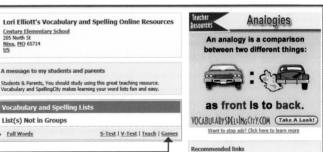

2. Let's take a look at the spelling test option. When a student clicks on *S-Test*, she'll hear the first spelling word recited and used in a sentence.

3. To hear the word repeated, the student can click on the button labeled *Say It*. To hear the sentence again, the student can click on the button labeled *Sentence*.

4. After the student types the word, she'll need to click the mouse on the next line to continue. When the student is finished with the test she must click on *Check Me!* at the bottom of the screen.

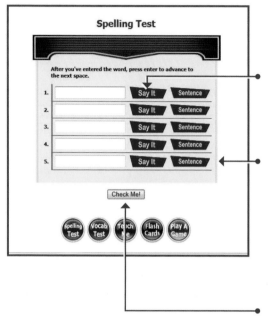

POST-TEST OPTIONS

1. A pop-up window will show the student her test results. The student can click on the *Teach Me* button next to any missed words to review them.

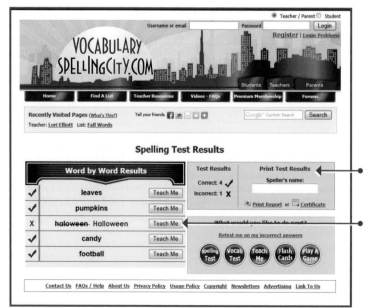

2. On the right-hand side of the screen is a blue box. The student can type in her name and then click on *Print Report* or *Certificate*.

3. A report will give a detailed list showing which words the student spelled correctly and which ones were missed.

4. The certificate is an official-looking document signed by the mayor of VocabularySpellingCity announcing the percentage of words the student spelled correctly.

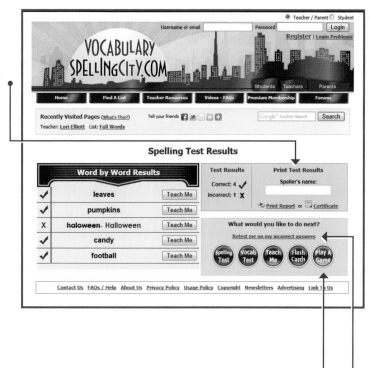

5. Notice the yellow box on the bottom right-hand side. A student can click on *Retest me on my incorrect answers*, or choose from the other options listed on colored circles.

PLAY A SPELLING GAME

1. What does it look like if a student chooses to play a game? When the student clicks on the green *Play a Game* circle, a screen of game choices will appear. These games take your spelling words and put them in various game formats.

2. The student must choose from the games listed on the left-hand side of the screen under *Free Activities*.

3. One of my favorite games is *HangMouse*. Students must guess letters and try to spell a word before the cat wakes up.

4. The interactive nature, immediate feedback, and self-checking features of VocabularySpellingCity make this both a valuable and favorite resource for teachers and students.

Look What You Can Do

VocabularySpellingCity makes differentiating spelling instruction a breeze. After pre-assessing students with a spelling inventory test, you can create customized weekly lists to meet the needs of each student. For example, you may have a group of students that requires a shorter list, another group that would benefit from the challenge of more complex words, and a group of English language learners who needs lists that focus on basic words. This site is also perfect to use with struggling learners during tutoring sessions. The games provide the fun and novelty, and you provide the instruction.

You can structure your week to keep students accountable by assigning an online VocabularySpellingCity activity for each day of the week. For example:

Monday	Take pre-test using the *Spelling Test* option and practice missed words using the *Teach Me* feature
Tuesday	Play HangMouse or Sentence Unscramble (found in the *Play a Game* feature)
Wednesday	Alphabetize Words (found in the *Play a Game* feature)
Thursday	Practice sentence or paragraph writing (found in the *Play a Game* feature)
Friday	Take Spelling Test and print results

Get Real

What if a student doesn't have access to the Internet at home? Many of the spelling games have a printing option. For example you can print a copy of the Alphabetize or Unscramble activities. Sending home print-outs is a helpful option for those students who don't have Internet access at home.

This site will not and should not replace our instruction of spelling or words. It's meant to be used as a supplement. Helping students understand word parts, defini-tions, and word usage within their own writing is still very important. Vocabulary SpellingCity focuses on correct spelling of words within sentence context. It's a great tool for students because it gives them the practice they need in a novel way. But the best way for students to learn spelling is through the process of creating their own writing.

A QUICK TIP

This is a great resource to use for administering spelling testing because the technology does the work for you. Students can use headphones to listen to the words, take the tests online, and then print out their graded results. So easy!

Incorporating Project-Based Learning

Is it your year to have "the class?" By this I mean a group of children tagged with descriptions like behavior issues, strugglers, or odd ducks. If you teach long enough, you'll eventually get "the class." I have to admit I love those kids. They're challenging, yet precious. One year I had "the class" in fourth grade. I knew they were going to be a handful before I even met them because everyone had shared that information with me. I was prepared. I even shortened my maternity leave so I could be there as much as possible. I felt that if I lost them in the first weeks of school I'd never get them back. Who needs six weeks to recover? Two will be just fine. I pause here to state that was probably one of the dumbest things I have ever done, but somehow I survived.

I've always loved teaching hands-on, but with this group of students, that style of teaching became a must. Worksheets and busywork would have never cut it with that bunch. The more they could build, create, and experience the better. The one thing that struck me early in the year was their limited background of experiences. Most of the children were from poor homes or dysfunctional families. These kids had not been on vacations. Their parents had not read with them or taken them to museums. It was clear to me that I was going to have to not only teach the curriculum but build background knowledge for everything. The more real-world connections I could make for them, the more willing they would be to focus and learn.

The Importance of Constructing Meaning

By early spring I had seen growth, but I knew I was going to send them on to the next grade soon and I was worried. I wanted them to succeed not just in fourth grade, but in life. Perhaps many of them would never go to college, but I wanted to instill in them the belief that they could be achievers. I looked over the curriculum left to cover and started to see connections. I had measurement, geometry, and simple machines left to teach. I decided that we would build a playhouse to help "the class" learn those things. Not a model of a playhouse but one that would be used on our playground.

It was crazy. I knew nothing about architecture, building, or tools. But I knew friends who were experts in those fields, and there were parents of my students who had those skills. We all joined together to make it happen. The students drew up plans, and we voted on our favorite. We wrote letters and made visits to local businesses to ask for donations and supplies. The students measured, drilled, and nailed the pieces together. Parents and friends spent their evenings and Saturdays helping us finish the construction. Somehow by the end of the school year, the playhouse was completed, painted, and placed in a special spot on the playground. At the dedication, you have never seen more proud and smiling kids than "the class." No other students had ever done such a thing, and, honestly, no other group ever would. It was the most project-based learning experience I've ever organized.

Years have gone by since that experience, but those students still talk about building the playhouse. They've moved on to college and careers, but the memory and the learning stay with them and me.

Meeting the Challenges of the 21st-Century Workplace

This example is not to say every teacher should have fourth graders grab a hammer and get busy. Not at all. The message instead is about the power of using project-based learning experiences and real-world applications to teach the curriculum. Today's world is more global and collaborative in nature than ever before. Most 21st-century jobs require people to work with others to solve problems and create new things. How can we prepare our students to succeed in that world when we don't even know what it's going to look like in the next five years? Technology really is changing everything that radically and that rapidly.

What I've found is that it's not just "the class" that needs project-based learning. It's every class. I believe we can best prepare our students if we offer them real learning experiences and teach them to think. Instead of building a playhouse, students can use online tools and experiences to connect and collaborate with others. Let me share with you some ways you can bring that approach into your classroom without having to pick up a saw and drill.

In the pages that follow, I'll introduce you to inquiry-based lessons called WebQuests, which provide students with hands-on, problem-based challenges. Your students must collaborate with other students to solve those problems and create a product to show what they know. I promise you, the learning is powerful. I'll also show you an online tool called Zunal that will help you to design and publish your own WebQuest. Finally, I'll show you how to get your class involved in online collaborative projects. You and your students will reach outside of your classroom to work with other students around the country and the world. Talk about preparing your students to meet the challenges of the 21st-century workplace! Not only will your students get the opportunity to learn new skills, they'll actually interact with a global community. Sound exciting? It is, and your students will think so, too.

Journey into WebQuests & Zunal

Quest is a great word, don't you think? The word is synonymous with an expedition or a journey. How often are we able to take our students on a learning expedition these days? Consider the obstacles. Lack of funding, strict curriculum, and time restraints are just a few of the reasons not to stretch beyond the norm. But what if you found a way to teach your curriculum in an intriguing way that used time wisely, wouldn't cost a dime, and taught your students to use 21st-century learning skills? Would you be interested?

Let me introduce you to WebQuests, an inquiry-based project wherein students use websites and web tools to solve real-world problems. Everything students need to complete the project is organized online. A high-quality WebQuest requires research, collaboration with others, critical thinking, and the production of an authentic artifact to showcase learning.

Let me give you an example. One of the most memorable Web-Quests I've used with my students was called Trading Spaces. The *Trading Spaces* television show was popular a few years ago, and students could relate to the idea of people swapping houses and redecorating for their friends. The WebQuest I used paired students. Each student's task was to design the perfect bedroom for his partner. Because the students were connected to the task, they were eager to find a solution.

Students had to interview their partners, create designs using geometry concepts, create a design board, build a 3D model, stay within an imaginary budget, and present the final product to the class. It was an amazing experience. When I realized how much curriculum my students were learning while being absolutely glued to their work, I was ecstatic. They learned language arts, math, science, social studies, and art content, plus they developed technology skills such as researching using online tools, creating graphs and charts with software, and making presentations using PowerPoint. Are you ready for the fun? Let the quest begin.

Let's Get Started

WebQuests take time. They aren't designed to be accomplished in one class period. They usually take two to six weeks to finish. It's not that you work solely on the WebQuest during those weeks, but rather it replaces the time spent in, say, the science or social studies or part of your language arts block. The best way I can explain a WebQuest is to take a look at one with you.

THE COMPONENTS OF A WEBQUEST

1. A colleague of mine has graciously allowed me to share her WebQuest with you. It is called Ecosystems WebQuest, and she designed it for use with her fourth-grade students.

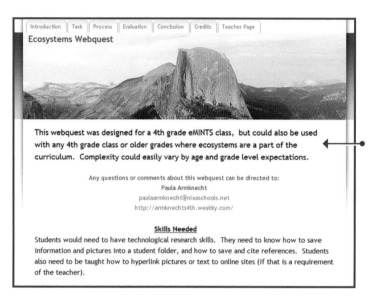

2. Every WebQuest should have the following components: Introduction, Task, Process, Evaluation, and Conclusion. Notice each of those components listed in the tabs across the top of her WebQuest page.

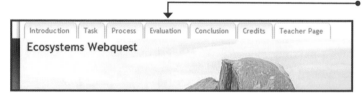

3. Now let's take a closer look and see how she set up her WebQuest.

INTRODUCTION

1. The Introduction to a WebQuest should hook students from the beginning. Its purpose is to set up the scenario or background for the WebQuest.

2. In the example, students are being encouraged to submit an article to a national magazine about a fascinating location in the world. A good introduction, like this one, will get students excited about the project.

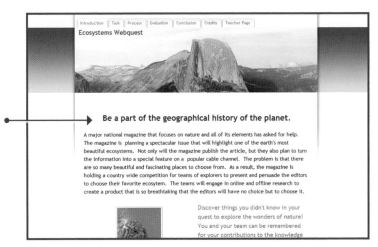

TASK

1. The Task outlines for students what specific problem they need to solve or what role they must assume to complete an important job. The Task also lets the students know what product they must create to showcase their findings.

2. Students involved with the Ecosystems WebQuest will work in teams of four and create a presentation to share with the class.

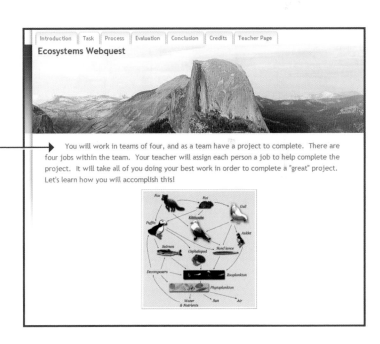

PROCESS

1. Process provides the scaffolding for learning, or steps in the process necessary to complete the task. It should also provide the online resources needed to complete the quest. Students should not just randomly search for information online.

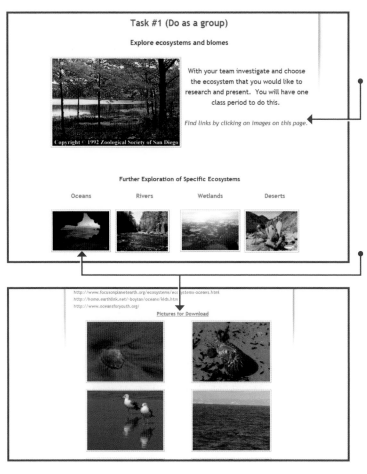

2. In the example, the students find research links by clicking on the images of the various ecosystems seen on the page.

3. Once they click on a picture, students are taken to a resource page that includes links and images they can use for their projects. In this example, students chose Oceans.

EVALUATION

1. The Evaluation component is really beneficial for teachers because it provides us with a rubric for scoring the project. If there are multiple parts to the WebQuest, there should be multiple rubrics or evaluation tools.

2. In the example, students will be scored both as team members and individually.

CONCLUSION

1. The conclusion summarizes what students should expect to learn by completing the WebQuest. It should also provide additional information to extend the learning.

2. In the example, students are provided with more links to visit and are encouraged to continue their learning.

TEACHER PAGE

1. Along with the five basic parts of a WebQuest, many teachers add a Teacher Page. The intent of this page is to help other teachers understand what prior knowledge and skills students might need in order to successfully participate in the WebQuest.

2. Teachers often outline the grade levels the WebQuest was designed for, the learning standards it addresses, tips for management, and a timeline for planning.

What will you get from this project?

At the conclusion of your team's research and presentation, each of you will have a better understanding of the natural world and your part in preserving it for the future. You will more fully appreciate the beautiful and diverse ecosystems and biomes on earth, and will understand how even the most harsh and extreme environments contain life. Who knows? You might just find your life's calling as a biologist or environmentalist. You will most definately be proud of your own use of technology in accomplishing this learning task. Congratulations!

You may even find that a career in biology, geology, zoology, botany, or meteorology may be of interest to you. If you think that you would like to investigate one of these careers, here are links that will give you more information:

http://www.ametsoc.org/pubs/careers.html
http://animaldiversity.ummz.umich.edu/site/index.html
http://www.fieldmuseum.org/research_collections/botany/default.htm
http://www.exploratorium.edu/explore/index.html

Introduction | Task | Process | Evaluation | Conclusion | Credits | Teacher Page

Ecosystems Webquest

This webquest was designed for a 4th grade eMINTS class, but could also be used with any 4th grade class or older grades where ecosystems are a part of the curriculum. Complexity could easily vary by age and grade level expectations.

Any questions or comments about this webquest can be directed to:
Paula Armknecht
paulaarmknecht@nlxaschools.net
http://armknechts4th.weebly.com/

Skills Needed
Students would need to have technological research skills. They need to know how to save information and pictures into a student folder, and how to save and cite references. Students also need to be taught how to hyperlink pictures or text to online sites (if that is a requirement of the teacher).

3. I hope from my colleague's example you can see how the creativity of a teacher and the structured format of a WebQuest can be used to help students succeed.

Where to Find WebQuests

But where can you find good WebQuests for your students? I have some excellent sites for you to visit. Let's start at the source. Bernie Dodge, PhD, professor of educational technology at San Diego State University developed the model for WebQuests in 1995. He has a site called Quest-Garden where teachers can post their WebQuests to share with others.

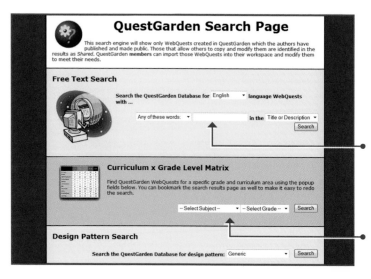

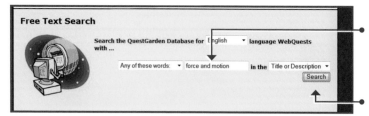

Status	Name & Description	Design Pattern	Grade/Content Areas	Reading Grade Level
Shared	**Motion and Force** This Webquest will provide sources of information for the student to analyze the relationship between motion and the forces that effect motion, and demonstrate their knowledge by designing a roller coaster ride. *Last published: Aug 29, 2010 Word count: 988*	GENERIC	Grade: 6-8 Science	8.3
Shared	**Force and motion** showing children how, when blown on, move different objects.rocks, feathers, cotton ball, etc. Also to teach children how these objects react to the force. *Last published: Jun 27, 2006 Word count: 549*	CC	Grade: K-2 Science	2.0
Shared	**Rockin' and Rollin' with Force and Motion** This webquest allows students to use their knowledge of force and motion to design a rollercoaster. *Last published: Jul 8, 2011 Word count: 611*	0	Grade: K-2 Science	5.3
Shared	**Let The Force Be With You** Let the Force be with you!!! *Last published: Jul 5, 2007 Word count: 247*	REC	Grade: 3-5 Science	4.2
Shared	**May The FORCE Be With You!!** Students will explore the concepts of forces and motion. In this webquest, they will learn about Newton's three laws of motion and the factors that affect motion. *Last published: Oct 25, 2008 Word count: 2129*	GENERIC	Grade: 3-5 6-8 Math Science	8.2
Shared	**May The Force Be With You!!!** The purpose of this WebQuest is to expose students to the properties of magnets and permit them to explore and discover how magnets work through attraction and repelling. *Last published: Nov 30, 2005 Word count: 432*	0	Grade: 3-5 Science	6.5
Shared	**Force (Luke Gasper)**	GENERIC	Grade: 9-12	7.2

QUESTGARDEN

1. Go to http://questgarden.com/. There will be a menu on the left, click on *Search for Examples.*

2. On the new page that loads, use the first yellow box to search the database for WebQuests by topic. Or use the gray box to search for WebQuests by subject or grade level.

3. For example, let's say I'd like to use a WebQuest to help me teach force and motion. I would type in "force and motion" and then click on the *Search* button.

4. Next, I'd scroll through the WebQuests to find one that matches my grade level and will be interesting to my students. There's a range of quality on QuestGarden, so be sure all the components of a good WebQuest are present.

eMINTS

1. Another place to find great WebQuests is at eMINTS, which stands for enhancing Missouri's Instructional Networked Teaching Strategies. The site provides teachers with instructional models that incorporate high-quality lesson design, inquiry-based learning, and technology.

2. Go to http://www.emints.org/inside-emints/webquests/. Scroll down the page and click on *WebQuests Created by eMINTS Teachers.*

3. Click on a WebQuest title to view it. The Web-Quests are listed by subject area and grade level.

4. Under *Grades 3–5 Mathematics*, you'll find the Trading Spaces WebQuest that I mentioned earlier in this chapter.

5. eMINTS teachers submit their WebQuests to the site to be posted. Each submission is scored very rigorously. Only those that are exceptional make it to the site. This helps tremendously when you're looking for the best options available.

Look What You Can Do

Maybe you would like to create your own WebQuests for students to use. You may already have a great project you do and you think it would fit nicely into the WebQuest format. Some teachers use blogs or websites to make their WebQuest. These are easy formats to work with because you can design the tabs for each section of the WebQuest. The sample ecosystem WebQuest discussed earlier in the chapter was created using the free website maker Weebly (see pages 69–79). Zunal is an online tool that's designed to help you create your own WebQuest.

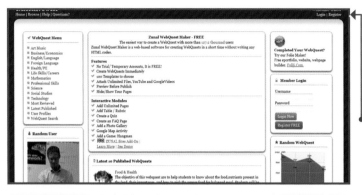

ZUNAL

1. Go to http://zunal.com/ to set up a free account. Look at the top right-hand corner of the page and click on *Register*.

2. In the Registration box, type in your name, gender, country, e-mail, username, and password. Click on the blue *Create Account* button when you're finished.

3. You'll see a *Registration Successful* message next. Click on the blue text that says *Click Here* to access your account.

4. Next you'll need to log in using your username and password. Click the blue *Login* button when you're finished.

5. Since you don't have a WebQuest in your account yet, click on the blue text that says *Create a New WebQuest*.

6. Since you're using the free account, you'll need to create a WebQuest from scratch. Click on the blue button that says *Create a New WebQuest from Scratch*.

CREATE YOUR PAGES

1. The first step is to give your WebQuest a title. Type your title in the empty box. Click the blue *Save Now* button when you are finished.

2. That was fast! The next screen will show you that pages have been created for your WebQuest. Click on the *Continue* button to add details to your pages.

3. I gave my WebQuest the title "Be a Detective." To add details to a page, you must first open that page. Notice the menu on the left-hand side of the screen. If you want to work on the *Process* page of your WebQuest, click on the green *Process* button.

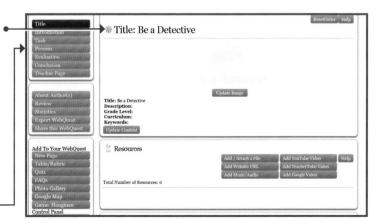

ADD TEXT

1. See the box with all of that really small text? It's full of helpful hints on what to include on your page. Under the box is an *Update Content* button. Click on that button.

2. A box will pop up for you to type in your information. Click *Save Now* when you're done.

ADD PHOTOS, LINKS & MORE

1. To add a photo, click on the *Update Image* button.

2. A pop-up window will open. Click on the *Browse* button.

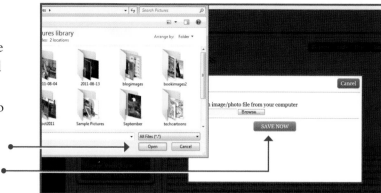

3. Find the folder where you save your images and double click on it. Click on the photo you'd like to select, and then click the *Open* button. Then click *Save Now* on the Zunal screen.

4. Now look to the bottom right-hand side of the screen. Notice the gray buttons. For each page in your WebQuest, you can click on a button to add a file, videos, or music, or link to a website.

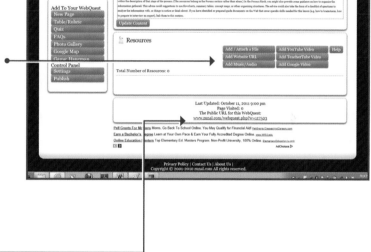

5. Use the steps described above to complete each section of your WebQuest. It's that simple. When you're done, scroll to the bottom of any one of your pages. In purple text you'll find your *Public URL* for the WebQuest.

GET YOUR LINK

1. The *Public URL* is the link others will need to locate your WebQuest. This doesn't mean it's public to everyone, just those who know this link. You'll want to give this link to your students.

2. I suggest you paste the link to your blog or website, save it as a Favorite on your computer, or save it as an icon on your desktop. To learn how to link to a website created on Weebly, see page 77. To learn how to save a link as an icon on your computer's deskstop, see page 43.

3. At the top of the page, there's a gray *Preview Mode* button in the top right-hand corner. You can click this to see your WebQuest as the students will see it.

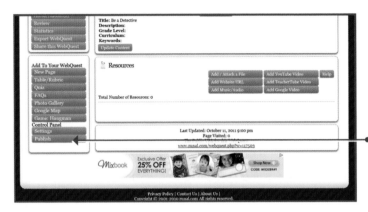

PUBLISH YOUR WEBQUEST

1. When you're all finished creating your Web-Quest, go to the bottom left-hand side of the screen and click on the gray *Publish* button.

2. Look across the new page and click again on the gray *Publish* button. Con-gratulations! Your Web-Quest is now available to be seen and used by your students when they type in the website address you pro-vided them.

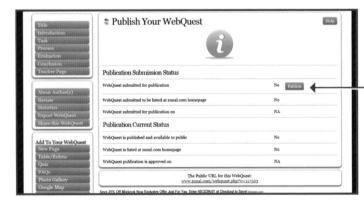

3. If you want to submit your WebQuest to Zunal's database so others can search and find your WebQuest on the Zunal site, then you'll need to complete the next screen in the Publish process.

4. Next to where it says *WebQuest submitted to be listed at zunal.com home page,* click on *Submit.* Zunal doesn't actually score the WebQuests, but they do look for completed projects and appropriateness before publishing.

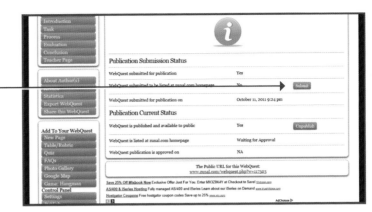

5. Not so bad, right? I thought you would be impressed with how simple this was to use. With Zunal, your quest continues.

Get Real

Here's a note about adding text to a page on Zunal. The program won't let you simply copy and paste text from Word, so if you've typed your work into a Word document first, you'll either need to retype your text or use a program called Notepad. Go to your Programs and type "Notepad" in the Search bar to see if you are already equipped with the program (it's included on Windows 7). If you don't have it on your computer, you can download it for free at http://notepad-plus-plus.org/. Now all you have to do is copy and paste your text into the Notepad program, and it'll convert the text into the form Zunal requires.

The free subscription of Zunal limits you to one WebQuest per account. You can have multiple accounts using different e-mail addresses, but plan accordingly if you want to create several WebQuests.

The first bit of reality I should address is the possibility and probability that you won't have computers for each of your students to use to complete a WebQuest. It's not necessary for students to each have a computer of their own to work on a WebQuest. In fact, having students work in pairs is actually better because of the collaboration. Use a computer lab, mobile lab, or rotate students on the one or two computers in your classroom.

When I first started using WebQuests, I only had my teacher computer, a projector, and a SMART Board. I brought in an old computer from home without Internet access for students to use. It was pretty

A QUICK TIP

Teachers are now being encouraged to integrate mobile devices into their WebQuest projects. Grab more ideas for using mobile devices to enhance your WebQuests by viewing Bernie Dodge's presentations at http://www.slideshare.net/bdodge/presentations/.

bare bones. I used the projector to show the WebQuest and go over the components with students. In addition to the online resources, I organized a cart of books and other resource materials for students to use. I made the class computer available and rotated groups of students to the SMART Board to use the online resources. For the creation of products, I included nontechie options as well as digital options. It takes a little more planning and scheduling, but it's possible to do a WebQuest with limited technology. It's not the best scenario, but it is doable.

One other thing I'd share from my experience with WebQuests is the importance of finding a quality one. Many people post WebQuests online that either don't fit the true structure of a WebQuest or are simply read-and-answer-the-question types of activities using the computer. The purpose of a Web-Quests is to develop higher-order thinking strategies, so stay away from less than stellar WebQuests. Also, choose one that will appeal to your students. If the task isn't realistic or interesting enough, students will moan and groan their way through the process. Sometimes people write WebQuests that are so unrealistic a student thinks, "This could never happen in real life, so why are we doing this?" To break it down even further, if the WebQuest is lame, don't use it.

Engage Students in Online Collaborative Projects

Eight teachers, one hallway, yards of butcher paper, and giggles all around. That's how I remember the fun times when my colleagues and I worked together to make our area of the building look like an entirely different place. Together we constructed a cave, a log cabin, and even a winter wonderland. But there could be nothing more spectacular than seeing the students' eyes light up when they walked into the magical worlds we created.

There's something very special about being part of a group on a mission. When everyone's working together with the same goal in mind, it's inspiring. There's such a feeling of pride and accomplishment when the task is completed. I want my students to experience the joy of working with others for that specific reason. That's why I love incorporating online collaborative projects into my curriculum each year.

When involved in an online collaborative project, students use Internet resources to share their learning with others living in different locations. All participants are learning the same content and then sharing their results online. When participating in an online project, students connect with other students from around the globe to pursue the same goals. Talk about teaching 21st-century learning skills! Collaborating on a project that extends outside the walls of your school will certainly help your students to develop a global view of the world.

So how do you get started? Where do you find online projects? And do you need to be a real techie in order to participate? I think you'll be pleasantly surprised to learn that no matter what your level of technical expertise, you can be successful. Participation in an online project is free, and the creators of high-quality collaborative projects will help guide you through the process step-by-step. I'm pleased to be able to share some of my favorite sites and resources for online collaborative projects with you.

Let's Get Started

There are many different kinds of online collaborative projects. Some take place on one particular day of the year such as Read Across America

Day, while others take place all year long like the Teddy Bears Around the World Project. Most online projects, however, are scheduled for a certain time period within the school year such as the O.R.E.O. Project. Interested teachers register for a specific online project and then are provided the tools and timeline to complete the task.

An important part of participation in an online project is the responsibility of sharing the results or products that are created. I think this will be much easier to understand if I show you a couple of examples in more detail.

CYBERBEE

1. I've been involved with online projects for years now, and I love the whole notion of my students connecting with other students who are engaged in the same learning experience at the same time.

2. Two projects that have been very successful with my students are Postcard Geography and Westward Ho, projects created, organized, and managed by teachers at CyberBee.

3. Each year CyberBee provides different opportunities for students to collaborate with others. For the latest opportunities visit http://www.cyberbee.com/projects.html.

POSTCARD GEOGRAPHY

1. Postcard Geography usually spans three or four months. Classes register to participate and then exchange picture postcards of their schools and locations. It's an amazing way for students to learn about other places around our country or world.

2. It's a class-to-class exchange. You can send digital or traditional postcards. I used the theme Goofin' Around the Globe with this project. As we received postcards, we added them to the display.

3. The students loved creating postcards both online and by hand. Postcards can be made on the computer and mailed, created and sent through e-mail, hand drawn, or commercially purchased and sent. Getting mail was never so exciting.

4. Students learned a lot about the different regions of the country and about the 50 states.

5. Students completed their postcards during Writer's Workshop throughout the weeks, so they had a real purpose for writing.

6. See how easy that was. We're all familiar with postcards in some format, so this is a very doable first project.

WESTWARD HO!

1. Another memorable online project is the Westward Ho journey.

2. My students and I have participated in this one for several years. This project takes place over two months, and students all over the country gather together to travel west as pioneers.

3. This is the ultimate simulation for learning. Groups of students pretend to be pioneer families. They face challenges along the trail and must make joint decisions. Their fates depend on how well they research each situation and choose directions.

Pioneer Days 2008

4. There are wonderful online experiences, such as a Trading Post where families buy and trade supplies and the Bulletin Board families use to post messages to other pioneers.

5. The Wagon Mistress also organizes real-time fireside chat sessions for everyone to participate and discuss the journey.

6. Students keep journals of their trip; use math skills to keep their families stocked with supplies and stay within budget; learn about weather and landforms as they go across country; and, of course, they develop a strong understanding of the historical period.

7. This project is always a highlight in the school year. Every subject area is integrated into the process. It's the best!

PROJECTS BY JEN

1. To summarize so far, a good online collaborative project is linked to content, has high interest for students, is organized, and leads the participants step-by-step through the process.

2. Now that you have a better understanding of the concept of online projects, let me show you some more places to find quality experiences.

3. Check out Projects by Jen at http://www.projectsbyjen.com/. This site is designed for PreK to sixth-grade students. Once you're at the home page, click on the green *Projects* tab.

4. Each school year a calendar of projects is listed with the dates for registering. Browse through the list of projects, taking note of the time frames. Consider which topics best match your grade level and curriculum.

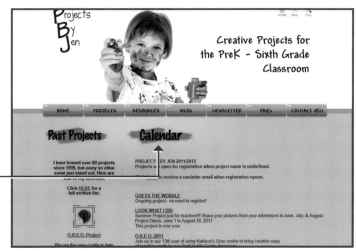

5. Over the years there have been projects based on holidays, foods, historical events, and favorite books. Each project will provide you with activities, lessons, and requirements.

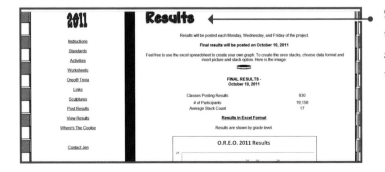

6. One of the most popular projects each year is the annual O.R.E.O. Project, wherein students use their critical thinking skills and fine motor skills to stack as many Oreo cookies as possible before they tumble.

7. Notice the navigating tools on the left- hand side of the page. Here you'll get the *Instructions*, *Standards*, *Activities*, *Results*, etc. for the project. I really appreciate and enjoy the framework that the author uses to organize each of her projects.

8. There are lesson activities for you to choose from in preparation of the actual cookie stacking.

9. There are pages for you to post and view the results at the end of the project time frame.

10. With all these helpful resources, everyone can participate in the project, even if you don't consider yourself to be very tech savvy. Think of how motivated your students will be when they know they are sharing their work with others from all over the country.

MORE RESOURCES FOR ONLINE COLLABORATIVE PROJECTS

1. The Center for Innovation in Engineering and Science Education showcases projects that work with real time data and collaboration. Their projects also align to national science and math standards.

2. For example, their Bucket Buddies project has students collecting samples from local ponds to answer the question: Are the organisms found in pond water the same all over the world?

3. Are you interested in learning more? Visit their site at http://www. k12science.org/.

4. The International Education and Resource Network is a nonprofit organization that enables teachers and students to connect with others across the world to collaborate on projects that enhance learning and seek to make a difference in the world.

5. To learn more about the IEARN, visit http://www.iearn.org/.

Look What You Can Do

Maybe you don't have lots of time to dedicate to a really involved online collaborative project. Then I'd encourage you to try a project that is specific to just one day.

Read Across America Day is a special day to honor Dr. Seuss. Students and teachers across the country read their favorite Dr. Seuss books and participate in activities. To learn more, visit http://www.seussville.com/Educators/educatorReadAcrossAmerica.php/.

Make math fun for your students by participating in World Maths Day. Students play math games

either at home or school. They compete against students from all over the world. They use their mental math skills to succeed. To learn more, visit http://www.worldmathsday.com/.

If you'd like to design your own online collaborative project, then check out ThinkQuest at http://www.thinkquest.org/en/.

ThinkQuest provides the platform for you to post your project and directions, and extend your project to other classrooms. It takes a few minutes to register, and your principal must also agree to the terms of the site, but it's a valuable tool for developing your own online collaborative projects.

A QUICK TIP

Journey North is one of the most successful online projects ever. The study of migration is the purpose of this project, and the journey of the monarch butterfly is highlighted. It's definitely a must to investigate. To learn more, visit Journey North at http://www.learner.org/jnorth/.

Get Real

A few words of advice before you decide to sign up for every online project you can find. First, realize each project takes time, and your participation is vital for the project to really be successful. I only tackle one or two projects a year. The projects I take on must align with my curriculum and be worth the time and effort. If it's a cute idea but doesn't have anything to do with my objectives, I have to pass. So choose wisely and don't over commit your class. Be reasonable about your schedule.

When you're involved with an online collaborative project make sure to get the word out. Let parents, colleagues, and the community know what you're doing. Everyone will be very impressed. Get a teacher buddy to take part in the project, too. It'll make you feel more comfortable, and it's nice to have someone to bounce ideas off of.

References

Andrade, H. 2007/2008. "Self-assessment through rubrics." *Educational Leadership,* 65(4): 60–63.

Boss, S. 2007. *Reinventing Project-Based Learning.* Eugene, OR: International Society for Technology in Education.

Dyches, T., N. Carter, and M. Prater. 2011. *A Teacher's Guide to Communicating with Parents.* Upper Saddle River, NJ: Pearson.

Elliott, L. 2011. *Teach Like a Techie.* Peterborough, NH: Crystal Springs Books.

Ferriter, B. 2009. "Taking the digital plunge." *Educational Leadership* 67(1): 85–86.

———. 2011. *Communicating and Connecting with Social Media.* Bloomington, IN: Solution Tree Press.

Gee, J. 2005. "Good video games and good learning." http://www.jamespaulgee.com/sites/default/files/pub/GoodVideoGamesLearning.pdf.

International Reading Association. 2009. "New literacies and 21st-century technologies." A position statement of the International Reading Association.

Jensen, E. 2008. "A fresh look at brain-based education." *Phi Delta Kappan* 89(6).

Kriete, R. 2002. *The Morning Meeting Book.* Turners Falls, MA: Northeast Foundation for Children.

March, T. 2005/2006. "The new www: whatever, whenever, wherever." *Educational Leadership* 63(4): 14–19.

Nielson, L., and W. Webb. 2011. *Teaching Generation Text*. San Francisco, CA: Jossey-Bass.

November, A. 2010. *Empowering Students with Technology*. Thousand Oaks, CA: Corwin.

Nussbaum-Beach, S. 2008. "No limits." *Technology and Learning* 28(7): 14–18.

Nussbaum-Beach, S., and L. Hall. 2011. *The Connected Educator: Learning and Leading in a Digital Age*. Bloomington, IN: Solution Tree Press.

Palfrey, J., and U. Gasser. 2008. *Born Digital: Understanding the First Generation of Digital Natives*. New York: Basic Books.

Prensky, M. 2010. *Teaching Digital Natives: Partnering for Real Learning*. Thousand Oaks, CA: Corwin.

Richardson, W. 2008. "Footprints." *Educational Leadership* 66(3): 16–19.

———. 2011. *Personal Learning Networks*. Bloomington, IN: Solution Tree Press.

Robinson, K. 2009. *The Element: How Finding Your Passion Changes Everything*. New York: Penguin Group.

Rosen, L. 2010. *Rewired: Understanding the iGeneration and the Way They Learn*. New York: Palgrave & Macmillan.

Sprenger, M. 2010. *Brain-Based Teaching in the Digital Age*. Alexandria, VA: ASCD.

Squire, K. 2011. *Video Games and Learning*. New York: Teachers College Press.

Tapscott, D. 2009. *Grown Up Digital: How the Net Generation Is Changing Your World*. New York: McGraw Hill.

Wittmann, L. 2010. *Clutter Rehab: 101 Tips and Tricks to Become an Organization Junkie and Love It*. Berkeley, CA: Ulysses Press.

Index